The Book Club Bible

The Definitive Guide
That Every Book Club Member Needs

Foreword by
LIONEL SHRIVER

MICHAEL O'MARA BOOKS LIMITED

First published in 2007 by
Michael O'Mara Books Limited
9 Lion Yard, Tremadoc Road
London SW4 7NQ

A CIP catalogue record for this book
is available from the British Library.

Papers used by Michael O'Mara Books Limited are natural,
recyclable products made from wood grown in sustainable forests.
The manufacturing processes conform to the environmental
regulations of the country of origin.

ISBN: 978-1-84317-269-7

1 3 5 7 9 10 8 6 4 2

Designed and typeset by Martin Bristow

Printed and bound in Great Britain
by Cox & Wyman, Reading, Berks

www.mombooks.com

Contents

Foreword

I own a threadbare T-shirt that says, 'Life's too short to drink bad wine.' An even savvier T-shirt would say, 'Life's too short to read bad books.' There really should be a word for that particular resentment you feel after ploughing through hundreds of pages that didn't pay off. A single reliable book recommendation can spare you hours of annoyance, impatience and disgust.

The Book Club Bible is like that one trustworthy friend upon whose taste you can pretty much rely. Dozens of my lifetime favourite reads appear in this guide, too many to itemize – although as a test I did check that one of my very, very favourite novels is indeed included (*The Age of Innocence* by Edith Wharton – see page 36). Usefully, this reference covers a wide range of both classics and popular fiction; you don't want to read only one or the other, any more than you'd want to dine day after day on steak alone, or on nothing but summer pudding. While about a third of these entries I haven't read myself, given the high quality of the selections that I have, I'm now putting the unread third on my private 'to do' list.

Though this guide is handy for individuals, it's obviously aimed at book clubs – about which, among the cultural elite, I sometimes detect a tinge of condescension. Maybe they just feel left out – and, in comparison to regular book club denizens, poorly read. Surely it's more stimulating to get together and talk about Kazuo Ishiguro's exquisite paean to servitude and emotional repression, *The Remains of the Day*, than to discuss kitchen remodelling, football scores or the state of the FTSE 100.

Book clubs often bring disparate people together, of different ages, ethnicities and outlooks. They help members get to know each other – and themselves – with a depth that chit-chat about property prices can't match. Was Anna Karenina really in love with Vronsky, or merely entranced by a romantic idea? You learn a lot about your own values when you try to reconcile sympathy for Yossarian's flight from the insanity of air force life with a moral discomfort over any Allied soldier going AWOL in the Second World War. (*Catch-22* – hilarious, and if you haven't devoured it already, a must-read.)

I consider the burgeoning popularity of book clubs one of the most encouraging social developments of recent times. Nothing delights me more in signing queues than when a boisterous cluster of readers declares that they had 'one of the best book club meetings ever' when discussing one of my novels. The claim consistently decodes: 'We got into a *huge* fight.' So the most fruitful selections for clubs aren't necessarily books that everyone loves, but especially the ones about which members violently disagree.

True, I spotted three or four selections included here (I won't say which) that I couldn't bear. But that just means that, at a book club meeting, I'd go bug-eyed with denunciation, and meanwhile three other folks would rail that it was one of the finest books they'd ever read. Someone tell Tony Bennett – *that*'s entertainment.

LIONEL SHRIVER, New York, 2007

Editors' Notes

- There's no wrong or right way to 'use' *The Book Club Bible*: you can skip straight to the books you've heard of, work your way through alphabetically, or concentrate on your favourite genre or author.

- In compiling the title selection, we made a rule that an author could be featured only once, and limited the choice to full-length books, so there are no plays, poetry or short stories.

- Each entry has been penned by a different writer, which accounts for the variations in style and approach.

- We've tried to include critical comments that go beyond gushing praise to something a little more thought-provoking.

- The book length provided relates to the edition the reviewer possessed; the number of pages may vary in other editions.

Introduction:
A Book Club Member Speaks

I belong to a book group that meets monthly, and over the last three years I've discovered some astonishing writing, made some good friends and quaffed plenty of wine. I've also enjoyed some furious debates – we've discussed gender politics, parental responsibility, deviant sexuality and the future of society. I have read and loved books I would never have chosen myself and heard fresh perspectives on some of my favourite novels.

Yet there is always a moment of agony at every meeting. *What shall we read next?* There is always a sinking feeling when you realize that the moment of choice has come round again and you can't *name* a single book, let alone suggest one that you would be happy to inflict on your book club and then discuss in detail. Add in the caprices of your group and it's a minefield.

This, then, is why you need this book. No longer will you flounder when asked to recommend a title. No longer will you propose a book only to find that there's not much to say about it, or that it simply wasn't the rapturous read it promised. The 100 entries in this book – and the themed 'top tens' – will provide inspiration.

Each featured title is described by a non-spoiler synopsis, so you can consider whether or not to read it without having the ending ruined. Furthermore, there are suggested discussion points to stimulate debate and abolish that dreadful pause at the beginning of every meeting. For those of you dedicated enough to read two books a time, or for those who wish to continue a debate at the next session that draws on a different writer's perspective, complementary titles are recommended.

This guide was well received by my book group. I wish you the same enjoyment in discovering stories that may change your world.

ANA SAMPSON, London, 2007

Things Fall Apart

CHINUA ACHEBE

Published 1958 / Length 148 pages

Things Fall Apart follows the ambitions and struggles of Okonkwo, a prominent member of a pre-colonial Igbo village in what is now Nigeria, as he strives to maintain his high standing within his community in the mid- to late-nineteenth century. Okonkwo has overcome a disadvantaged childhood to become a successful man, but he seems fated to lose the status he cherishes. His blind commitment to traditional values undermines his relationship with his family, particularly his son Nwoye. He is prepared to make great sacrifices in order to preserve his position in the village, yet Okonkwo's world is changing, as British colonial rule begins to encroach upon the Igbo way of life. Achebe portrays the colonial experience from an African perspective: the European culture promoted by the invading authorities represents a challenge to Okonkwo's identity, one he must overcome in order to survive. Written in the late 1950s against the backdrop of Nigeria's journey towards independence, the book raises questions about collective identity, morality and self-alienation, and constitutes the foundation of modern African literature in English.

WHAT THE CRITICS SAID

'Achebe is the conscience of African literature because he has consistently insisted on the power of storytellers to appeal to the morality and humanity of their readers and to give their life fuller meaning.' – SIMON GIKANDI, Professor of Literature, in his introductory essay to the Heinemann Classics in Context edition of the novel

DISCUSSION POINTS

- Okonkwo has been described as a classic tragic hero, but at times his actions make it difficult for the reader to identify with him. Why do you think Achebe makes his protagonist so morally ambiguous?

- How do the characters of Ezinma, Nwoye and Ikemefuna reflect the strengths and limitations of Igbo society?

- Why do you think Achebe includes descriptions of the more troubling Igbo customs, such as the abandoning of twin babies? Isn't there a danger of alienating Western readers from the society he is depicting?

- *Things Fall Apart* repeatedly emphasizes the importance of oral storytelling in Igbo culture. How does the telling of stories affect the way in which Achebe's novel is narrated?

BACKGROUND INFORMATION

- Achebe is an internationally renowned Nigerian academic who drew on his own family's experience of colonization to write this, his first novel. The story of Okonkwo's family is continued in *No Longer at Ease* (1960) and *Arrow of God* (1964).

- The title of the novel is taken from a line of W. B. Yeats's poem 'The Second Coming'.

- *Things Fall Apart* is the most widely read African novel and has been translated into fifty different languages, leading to Achebe being identified as the man who 'invented' modern African literature.

SUGGESTED COMPANION BOOKS

- *A Grain of Wheat* by NGUGI WA THIONG'O – detailing the effects of colonization on Kenyan identity during the 1952–60 Emergency.

- *The Tin Drum* by GÜNTER GRASS (see page 86) – exploring cultural alienation and the individual.

- *Baudolino* by UMBERTO ECO – the importance of storytelling.

Half of a Yellow Sun

CHIMAMANDA NGOZI ADICHIE

Published 2006 / Length 448 pages

Chilling violence erupted during the Nigeria–Biafra War, between 1967 and 1970, when the Igbo of eastern Nigeria sought to form an independent republic of Biafra; it is this important period of African history that is the focus of *Half of a Yellow Sun*. Adichie compellingly evokes the personal as well as the political, with three main characters at the heart of the story: Ugwu, a thirteen-year-old houseboy who spends his days scrubbing the floors and polishing the dishes of a university professor; the professor's beautiful lover Olanna, a young middle-class woman who has abandoned her privileged life in Lagos; and Richard, a shy Englishman who is bewitched by Olanna's twin sister. The novel depicts these characters' struggles as they are forced to test their ideals and loyalties under the shadow of the Nigerian troops' advance. As well as being an exploration of war and related issues such as moral responsibility and allegiance, this is at heart also a powerful love story.

WHAT THE CRITICS SAID

'Literary reflections on the Biafra war have a long and distinguished history, from the most famous poet to have died in the war, Christopher Okigbo, to Chinua Achebe, Cyprian Ekwensi and Flora Nwapa. Born in 1977, Adichie is part of a new generation revisiting the history that her parents survived. She brings to it a lucid intelligence and compassion, and a heartfelt plea for memory.' – *The Guardian*

DISCUSSION POINTS

- 'Perhaps he was not a true writer after all. He had read somewhere that, for the true writer, nothing was more important than their art, not even love.' Discuss the role of love and art in the novel. What impact does war have on them?

● The book takes its title from the emblem for Biafra, the breakaway state in eastern Nigeria that survived for only three years. What other significances do the images of sun, fire and light carry throughout?

● The novel begins in a time of peace before reaching war. How does this affect our response to the characters?

● Adichie uses the technique of a book within a book. What is the significance of this device?

BACKGROUND INFORMATION

● The novel won the 2007 Orange Prize for Fiction.

● In January 2004, Adichie was heralded by *The Washington Post Book World* as 'the twenty-first-century daughter of Chinua Achebe'.

● *Purple Hibiscus*, the author's first novel, won the 2005 Commonwealth Writers' Prize for Best First Book and the Hurston/Wright Legacy Award. It was also shortlisted for the 2004 Orange Prize and the John Llewellyn Rhys Prize, and longlisted for the 2004 Booker Prize.

SUGGESTED COMPANION BOOKS

● *Things Fall Apart* by CHINUA ACHEBE (see page 10) – a classic account of a changing Nigeria.

● *Surviving in Biafra* by ALFRED OBIORA UZOKWE – a memoir of civil war seen through the eyes of a young boy.

● *The Icarus Girl* by HELEN OYEYEMI – a novel set partly in Nigeria.

● The *Regeneration* trilogy by PAT BARKER – exploring the effect of war on civilian life.

Brick Lane

Monica Ali

Published 2003 / Length 492 pages

An enjoyable and inspiring read, *Brick Lane* contains a potpourri of archetypal modern characters caught in a morass of angst and alienation. Nazneen is an eighteen-year-old woman wrenched from her family and the relative security of her Bangladeshi village to be married off to a man old enough to be her father, and forced to live in London, a place she doesn't know. Chanu, her husband, a man who came to Britain expecting to get on if he worked and studied hard, has learned the hard way that Britain isn't quite the land of golden opportunity it appeared to be from Bangladesh. For years, Nazneen keeps house, looks after her husband, bears his children and dutifully maintains her horizons within her home and family. When reality finally dawns on Chanu, with it comes the realization that he cannot earn enough to support his family. Suddenly, Nazneen's world broadens, and with the purchase of a second-hand sewing machine and an introduction to Karim, a young second-generation British-Bangladeshi, her life changes for ever.

READER'S OPINION

'Ali lifts the lid on contemporary immigrant life in modern urban Britain. It's both surprising and heart-warming and gives a real sense of the fractured identities that so many immigrant people and especially their children are trying to forge into a coherent whole. Excellent.' – MIKE, 37

DISCUSSION POINTS

- How successful is Ali at conveying the alienation felt by her characters, both towards each other and within the society in which they find themselves?

- For what audience is this book primarily written? Do you think it helps to foster better understanding and respect between indigenous and immigrant people?
- How is hypocrisy handled in the book? In particular, what do you make of Mrs Islam?
- Does the backdrop of escalating racial tension add to or get in the way of the other narratives?
- Should Western attitudes towards women and women's rights be overlaid on to different cultures, as here? Should we even ask that question?

BACKGROUND INFORMATION

- In 2004, Ali won the British Book Awards Newcomer of the Year and *Brick Lane* won the WH Smith People's Choice Award for Debut Novel. The book was also shortlisted for the Booker Prize, *The Guardian* First Book Award and the British Book Awards Literary Fiction Award.
- In 2003, *Granta* magazine named Ali as one of its twenty Best of Young British Novelists.

SUGGESTED COMPANION BOOKS

- *Straightening Ali* by AMJEED KABIL – a young British-born Pakistani man is forced into an arranged marriage by his family, even though they know he is gay.
- *The Buddha of Suburbia* by HANIF KUREISHI – Karim, a young English-Asian man living with his English mother and Indian father in south London, tries to find his own identity.
- *Small Island* by ANDREA LEVY (see page 132) – a Jamaican couple are befriended by their white landlady in post-war Britain, when to be black was to be a second-class citizen.

I Know Why the Caged Bird Sings

Maya Angelou

Published 1969 / Length 281 pages

I Know Why the Caged Bird Sings is the first volume in Maya Angelou's acclaimed series of autobiographies. Born Marguerite Johnson, she and her beloved brother, Bailey, are sent to live with their strict Southern Baptist grandmother in Stamps, Arkansas. The children call her Momma and her rules and religion bring an order to their young lives that their parents did not. Running the local store, Momma is in an unusual position during the troubled times in 1930s America, and she is able to protect her grandchildren from the harsher aspects of life during the Depression. The realities of growing up in the Southern states are painfully and truthfully depicted, but it is when the children are sent north to escape the potentially brutal attitudes of the white folks on the other side of town that Maya's life is turned upside down. Angelou's poetic writing style gives real depth to her descriptions of her formative years. She allows the reader genuine emotional access to the difficult and personal experiences of her childhood and adolescence, with moving and lyrical prose that manages to avoid self-pity, in a narrative that finishes on a note of hope.

Reader's opinion

'In her beautiful and honest account, Angelou confronts us with themes as huge and global as racial discrimination and as small and localized as a young girl's coming of age, each explored with equal poignancy and candour. An inspiring read.' – Anna, 20

Discussion points

● Maya spends much of her childhood with her grandmother in Arkansas – how does her strict upbringing contribute to her behaviour as she grows up?

- Following Maya's treatment at the hands of her mother's boyfriend, the family takes drastic action. How do you think young Maya's guilt over their protection of her affects her developing personality?

- How does her month of homelessness change Maya's outlook when she returns to her mother's home?

- Maya was almost completely mute for five years, yet she went on to become an eloquent speaker, civil-rights activist, poet, actress, dancer, playwright and university professor. Do you think her years of silence helped or hindered her transformation into the woman she became?

Background information

- The book's title comes from Paul Laurence Dunbar's poem 'Sympathy'.

Suggested companion books

- *The Color Purple* by ALICE WALKER (see page 212) – a woman finds the strength to overcome a horrendous childhood with the companionship of other women.

- *Beloved* by TONI MORRISON (see page 142) – a Pulitzer Prize-winning depiction of life at the end of slavery, and the extremes of motherly love.

- *Purple Hibiscus* by CHIMAMANDA NGOZI ADICHIE – examines the restrictions of a strict religious upbringing in a country undergoing dramatic political change.

Behind the Scenes at the Museum

KATE ATKINSON

Published 1995 / Length 382 pages

Populated with a large cast of vividly drawn characters, this bitter-sweet novel charts four generations of a Yorkshire family, focusing on the irrepressible Ruby Lennox, from her conception above a pet shop in 1952 to the present day. Narrated mainly in Ruby's engaging, witty voice, her family – the 'worn out', bitter mother, the roguish father, the eccentric sisters – are brought affectionately to life. Additionally, in a series of lengthy 'footnotes' inserted throughout the book, we learn the complex background of Ruby's family, taking in missing war heroes, absconding parents and numerous other family secrets. Tightly plotted with a satisfying ending, this is a book that demands close attention (some readers find the sheer number of characters confusing), yet its breezy style and wry humour make it a joy to devour quickly.

WHAT THE CRITICS SAID

'[An] offbeat, poignant and often playful first novel . . . But the majority of the [footnotes] (such as the one in which [Ruby's] grandmother buys new boots after the Boer War) do little to illuminate the more compelling modern-day narrative.' – *Salon*

DISCUSSION POINTS

- Did you find the book ultimately uplifting or depressing? If the former, how does the author achieve this, given the number of deaths and thwarted lives in the story?

- Ruby believes 'the past's what you take with you'. Do you think this is true, in terms of the novel? How are the various characters' lives affected by their family history?

- Do you think the book's complicated narrative structure is successful, or did you find it confusing? What are the advantages and disadvantages of this approach?

● Is there a common thread in the female personalities that runs through each generation of the family? Are the mother–daughter relationships believable?

● Kate Atkinson claimed in an interview that, among other things, the book is 'about cupboards – but no one seems to notice that!' What does she mean?

BACKGROUND INFORMATION

● *Behind the Scenes at the Museum* was Kate Atkinson's first book and won the Whitbread Book of the Year Award in 1995.

● Atkinson was inspired by a photo of her great-grandmother, and by the true story of the silver teaspoon (recounted in the third footnote).

SUGGESTED COMPANION BOOKS

● *After You'd Gone* by MAGGIE O'FARRELL – another debut novel of family secrets.

● *David Copperfield* by CHARLES DICKENS – *The Los Angeles Times* likened *Behind the Scenes at the Museum* to this nineteenth-century novel.

● *Oranges Are Not the Only Fruit* by JEANETTE WINTERSON – an unusual coming-of-age novel set in post-war northern England.

The Handmaid's Tale

MARGARET ATWOOD
Published 1985 / Length 324 pages

Set following violent wars between religious factions horrified at society's declining moral values, *The Handmaid's Tale* superbly illustrates the ways in which religious extremism might so easily turn the world upside down. Perhaps even more pertinent today than when it was written, Atwood's stark novel is set in the Republic of Gilead, formerly the United States, where, in a desperate attempt to increase the population, those women who are still fertile are enlisted as 'handmaids' and given to wealthy couples as surrogate mothers for their children. Each month, a ceremony is held between husband, wife and handmaid, literally interpreting a passage from the Bible in which the maid 'shall bear upon [the wife's] knees, that [she] may also have children by her'. Our heroine is the handmaid Offred – 'of Fred', named for the head of the household she is assigned to. In Gilead, the blame for infertility rests entirely with women. Offred must conceive this time, or face extradition and a certain death in the colonies. Although there is a degree of detachment from Atwood in developing her characters' personalities, she avoids leaving the reader cold by creating a gripping and nerve-racking narrative. She switches easily between Offred's present predicament and her memories, keeping the reader on edge until the very last page.

WHAT THE CRITICS SAID

'Margaret Atwood's terrain is sexual politics only, and within it, she strikes out on a broad front, not just against right-to-lifers, anti-ERA campaigners, born-again Christians, and Stepford Wives, but also against feminist puritans (Offred remembers make-up with forlorn longing), and essentialists who hymn childbirth, menarche [the first occurrence of menstruation] and sisterhood.' – *The Guardian*

Discussion points

- How does losing the right to use their own names affect the handmaids' sense of identity – existing only in terms of the man to whom they belong?

- Although Offred was once quite liberal herself, she now feels differently about her previous behaviour. How does the Gileadean regime so easily undo decades of progress in women's emancipation?

- Given the choice between the limited roles available to the female characters in *The Handmaid's Tale*, which route do you feel would be the best to take?

- In the novel, religious doctrine is taken from very specific passages of the Bible, and access to all literature is limited to the male head of each household. How does control over the written word change the balance of power between Offred and the Commander?

Background information

- Atwood is a Canadian author well known for her feminist writing. She won the 2000 Booker Prize for her novel *The Blind Assassin*.

- *The Handmaid's Tale* was the winner of the Arthur C. Clarke Award in 1987.

Suggested companion books

- *Nineteen Eighty-Four* by GEORGE ORWELL (see page 158) – a love story set in a totalitarian future state in which people are controlled by the original 'Big Brother'.

- *Brave New World* by ALDOUS HUXLEY (see page 114) – another dystopian future society imagined.

- *Mermaids in the Basement* by MARINA WARNER – another example of feminist literature, this short-story collection reworks folklore and legend.

The Wasp Factory

IAIN BANKS

Published 1984 / Length 184 pages

Sixteen-year-old Frank Cauldhame inhabits a remote Scottish island with his eminently dysfunctional 'family', which consists of his eccentric father and absent brother Eric. He presides over his territories through the observance of a macabre array of self-devised rituals, fixated on violence and death and self-consciously gothic in flavour. As Frank narrates his strange story, we learn some of the roots of this morbidity, and they make for uncomfortable reading. This is not a novel for the faint-hearted, but it is utterly gripping as Frank ushers us into the landscape of his twisted history and the protective, perverse mythology he has built around it. The wasp factory of the title is a bizarre mechanism constructed behind a salvaged clock face, in which live wasps 'choose' their bitter ends. Frank uses this apparatus as an oracle and talisman. He has never been in more need of its power as his estranged brother Eric closes in on the island and the Cauldhames still uneasily cohabiting there.

WHAT THE CRITICS SAID

'A silly, gloatingly sadistic and grisly yarn of a family of Scots lunatics . . . the lurid literary equivalent of a video nasty.' – *Sunday Express*

DISCUSSION POINTS

- There is a sensational twist in Frank's tale – did you anticipate this revelation? How does it retrospectively inform your reading of the book?
- What does Frank gain from his fetishistic totems and rituals?
- *The Wasp Factory* has been called a dark comedy – do you agree with this interpretation?

- Were Frank's actions 'just a stage [he] was going through', as he claims?

Background information

- *The Wasp Factory* was the prolific Iain Banks's first novel and generated critical controversy – it was variously acclaimed and viciously condemned by reviewers.
- The book was written during the years when Margaret Thatcher was Prime Minister, and it has been suggested that it describes the 1980s cult of the individual taken to an illogical and destructive extreme, in a similar vein to Bret Easton Ellis's *American Psycho*.
- The author also writes science-fiction novels under the name Iain M. Banks.

Suggested companion books

- *The Catcher in the Rye* by J. D. SALINGER (see page 180) – Holden Caulfield is the classic isolated adolescent.
- *Vernon God Little* by D. B. C. PIERRE (see page 166) – Booker Prize-winning meditation on disenfranchized youth, also blackly comic.
- *Morvern Callar* by ALAN WARNER – stunning portrait of a female Scottish outsider.
- *Robinson Crusoe* by DANIEL DEFOE – it has been suggested that *The Wasp Factory* is a retelling of Defoe's classic.

Light a Penny Candle

MAEVE BINCHY

Published 1982 / Length 600 pages

In this charming novel from one of the world's most beloved storytellers, themes of friendship, loneliness and honesty are sympathetically explored. Beginning in 1940 and spanning twenty years, *Light a Penny Candle* describes the childhood, adolescence and adulthood of Elizabeth White, a timid English girl, and Aisling O'Connor, a fiery and confident Irish lass, who are brought together when Elizabeth is sent to live with the O'Connors in Kilgarret for the duration of the Second World War. A lifelong friendship flourishes between the two, and as we follow the twists and turns of their stories against a backdrop of shifting social change, Binchy sheds light on the impact of life choices and how decisions may come back to haunt us. Narrated with humour as well as poignancy, it is a book about the things we don't say; the importance and limitations of family; the hurt and hope of relationships. It conveys an enduring faith in friendship, even after all other convictions have faded away.

WHAT THE CRITICS SAID

'Like so much of Maeve's output, *Candle* was regarded as unworthy of serious critical attention, even though several scenes in the novel . . . are Dickensian in their pathos.' – *The Independent*

DISCUSSION POINTS

- Think about the characters in the book. How do they change over the course of the novel? Are all the characters fully rounded, or does Binchy occasionally rely on stereotypes?

- 'It was going to be one long act from now to the very end.' This quotation could summarize the source of most major dilemmas in the novel. In what ways are the characters duplicitous to themselves and each other?

- To what extent is *Light a Penny Candle* a social commentary juxtaposing emotional, spiritual and financial poverty and wealth? What conclusions does it draw?

- The novel is firmly grounded in the social mores of the 1950s and 1960s. Does the story have impact only in this setting, or are its concerns still relevant in the modern day?

- There are a number of clear parallels in the narrative. Is this true to life or a literary construct? Can we help repeating the mistakes of others?

BACKGROUND INFORMATION

- Binchy is one of Ireland's most successful novelists, having sold over 40 million copies of her books in thirty languages worldwide.

- *Light a Penny Candle* was rejected four times by publishers – but Binchy eventually sold it for a £53,000 advance: the highest price ever paid in Britain for a debut novel at that time. It remained in the top ten for fifty-three weeks.

SUGGESTED COMPANION BOOKS

- *Sense and Sensibility* by JANE AUSTEN – features a friendship between two sisters with contrasting temperaments.

- *On Chesil Beach* by IAN McEWAN – a just-married young couple struggle to communicate in 1962.

- *The Pact* by JODI PICOULT (see page 162) – two lifelong friends who will do anything for each other . . . with fatal consequences.

Lorna Doone

R. D. BLACKMORE

Published 1869 / Length 624 pages

The stage on which this classic tale plays out is a gloomy Exmoor in the late seventeenth century, during the time of James II and the Monmouth Rebellion; an Exmoor pervaded by the menacing Doone clan. John Ridd, our hero, is twelve years old when the novel begins. His own father, a farmer, was murdered by Carver Doone, but what promises to be a story of revenge melts into epic romance as Ridd falls in love with the beautiful, aristocratic Lorna Doone. The novel explores the pain of wanting something beyond reach, forbidden passion and the extents to which one will go to save a beloved. Blackmore considers the redemptive power of love, examining whether it enables one to forgive even arch-enemies.

READER'S OPINION

'I read this book as a teenager and was gripped by its evocative setting, although I felt frustrated by the complicated plot and cheated by the ending. I recently tried to reread it as an adult and it wasn't quite as powerful.' – ANITA, 26

DISCUSSION POINTS

- 'This work is called a "romance", because the incidents, characters, time, and scenery, are alike romantic. And in shaping this old tale, the Writer neither dares, nor desires, to claim for it the dignity or cumber it with the difficulty of an historic novel.' This is how the author prefaces his work. Is *Lorna Dorne* a classic love story, or a piece of history? How do such categorizations help or hinder our appreciation of the story?

- How satisfying did you find the ending?

- What techniques does Blackmore use to build a sense of menace throughout the novel?

BACKGROUND INFORMATION

- The 1685 Monmouth Rebellion tried to overthrow King James II (who acceded to the throne after his brother, Charles II, died) in favour of James Scott, 1st Duke of Monmouth, an illegitimate son of Charles who claimed to be the rightful heir. It was a time of religious rivalries and great political unrest.

- *Lorna Doone* was first published anonymously in 1869 in a limited edition of just 500 copies, of which only 300 sold. The following year it was republished in one volume and has never since been out of print.

- The novel has inspired more than ten adaptations, including a 2000 BBC TV production. *Lorna Doone* also lends its name to a brand of shortbread.

SUGGESTED COMPANION BOOKS

- *Sir Gawain and the Green Knight* by an unknown author – a fourteenth-century verse romance set in King Arthur's time.
- *Rebecca* by Daphne du Maurier (see page 60) – another novel with a haunting geographical setting, in this case focusing not on Exmoor, but on du Maurier's native Cornwall.

Midwives

Chris Bohjalian

Published 1997 / Length 310 pages

One freezing winter night in 1981, a home birth goes badly wrong, and hippie Vermont midwife Sibyl Danforth is accused of killing her patient. As the legal system grinds into action, Sibyl is forced to contemplate a life without her calling, her family and her freedom. Yet this isn't Sibyl's story alone, although her diary entries are interspersed throughout. *Midwives* is narrated by her daughter, the watchful and ever curious Connie, who looks back on the life-changing events that happened when she was fourteen. Partly a tense courtroom drama, partly an introspective coming-of-age tale about the loss of innocence, *Midwives* is a compelling read, expertly woven with a strong sense of foreboding. The novel builds to an excruciating climax, and has enough power left to deliver a killer blow on the final page.

WHAT THE CRITICS SAID

'As with the Woodward affair [see BACKGROUND INFORMATION], several stories march hand in hand alongside the central question – did she or did she not kill? – which are stirred up into a nicely poisonous stew in order to flesh out a background of small-town politics and vested interests. They include a traditional north–south hostility, religious fundamentalism and the big battle between the medical orthodoxy which favours high-tech births in hospital and the smocked, peasant-frocked midwives who defend a woman's right to have her baby in her own home.' – *The Times*

DISCUSSION POINTS

● Is Connie a biased narrator? How would the book differ if Asa or Foogie narrated it?

- What is the effect of including Sibyl's diary entries, particularly the last entry in the book?
- Stephen always dresses 'one click above'. How important are external appearances in the book? Do you think Bohjalian exaggerates this for dramatic effect, or is it true to life?
- 'Lawyers have a language as cold as doctors.' Is it ultimately language that wins or loses this case?
- Is justice served? Does Connie do the right thing?

BACKGROUND INFORMATION

- The same year the book was published, the world was transfixed by the case of Louise Woodward, the British au pair accused of killing her eight-month-old charge in America, to which *The Times* compares the storyline of this book (the two are not directly linked).
- *Midwives* was selected for Oprah's Book Club in 1998.

SUGGESTED COMPANION BOOKS

- *Perfect Match* by JODI PICOULT – a book that is also centred on a fraught courtroom drama and a morally ambiguous death, and explores the impact that legal cases have on family life. Bohjalian is one of Picoult's favourite authors.
- *Atonement* by IAN MCEWAN (see page 134) – this novel features another child voyeur compelled to involve herself in adult machinations.
- *To Kill a Mockingbird* by HARPER LEE (see page 130) – legal complexities seen from the viewpoint of a child.

Any Human Heart

William Boyd

Published 2002 / Length 504 pages

Logan Mountstuart begins writing a private journal while still a seventeen-year-old schoolboy and continues it through other key phases of his varied and colourful life: as an Oxbridge student; then as a writer in 1930s London, meeting the rich and famous; through to his last years as a would-be recluse in rural France. In between, he is betrayed as a spy in the Second World War, enjoys the high life as a New York art dealer, and teaches English Literature at a university in Africa. Boyd captures both the tone of the man at different life stages and the mood of each historical period so convincingly that one feels genuine emotion for the fictional diarist. It is a book filled with love and war; success and tragedy; gains and losses in many forms. Throughout, Logan maintains his urge for adventure and a lifelong capacity for misjudgement. *Any Human Heart* is a riveting and inspiring ride through one man's life, taking in the changing landscape of the twentieth century along the way.

Reader's opinion

'Finishing this, I started to think seriously about my pension – even though I'm thirty years away from retiring. I was so galvanized, following this man's life. Just amazing. I cried after the epilogue, as if I knew him. Very odd.' – Simeon, 38

Discussion points

- In Mountstuart's 'Preamble' he writes that we 'keep a journal to entrap that collection of selves that forms us'. How, and how well, is this achieved in the journals that follow?

- Mountstuart accounts for his life and feelings in the present tense, sometimes in the heat of the moment. What are the implications of this? What might be different about a memoir looking back and reconstructing the material?

- How well does Boyd conjure up key trends in the almost-century spanned by the story?

- Reading these diaries, did you start to relate to Logan Mountstuart as you might an actual diarist – is Boyd successful here at the novelistic trick of suspending readers' disbelief?

- 'The view ahead is empty and void: only the view backward shows you how utterly random and chance-driven [life's] vital connections are.' Discuss, in light of both Mountstuart's experiences and Boyd's choice of narrative structure.

BACKGROUND INFORMATION

- Boyd introduced Logan Mountstuart in an earlier work, *Nat Tate: An American Artist 1928–1960*. Published in 1998, this 'biography' reportedly fooled several art critics, who expressed views on (the fictional) Nat Tate.

- *Any Human Heart* was shortlisted for the International IMPAC Dublin Literary Award in 2004.

- Boyd was appointed a CBE for services to literature in 2005.

SUGGESTED COMPANION BOOKS

- *My Century* by GÜNTER GRASS – a collection of stories set in Germany and spanning the twentieth century, in a series of narrative voices that include the autobiographical.

- *Oracle Night* by PAUL AUSTER – a moving portrayal of a writer's meanderings during his recovery from a near-fatal illness, with some literary playfulness thrown in for good measure.

The Thirty-Nine Steps

JOHN BUCHAN

Published 1915 / Length 138 pages

Richard Hannay's neighbour, Colonel Scudder, tells him of an anarchist plot to murder the Greek premier and tip Europe into war. When Hannay later finds Scudder dead, he thinks the police will accuse him of murder, and goes on the run. So begins Buchan's classic page-turner, which sees Hannay pursued by both the police and German spies through Galloway, Berkshire and Kent. Throughout this brief and gripping chase narrative, Hannay uses resource and cunning to avoid his pursuers. A certain suspension of disbelief is required to buy into the novel's close scrapes and unlikely coincidences. But disbelief duly suspended, you'll enjoy a fast-paced romp that helped shape the thriller genre, and a dashing spy-catcher who served as a prototype for countless heroes to come. And if some of Hannay's escapades seem a bit clichéd or old-fashioned now, it's only because Buchan's formula was so mercilessly aped by the writers who followed him.

READER'S OPINION

'Despite its archaic tone, the novel was enjoyable, and had enough twists and turns to keep me involved. The character of Richard Hannay was a bit two-dimensional, though. He just seemed to be a straightforward hero with no weaknesses.' – COLLETTE, 28

DISCUSSION POINTS

- The novel is often classified as 'genre' fiction rather than serious literary fiction. Is there really such a difference between the two?
- How are the upper and lower classes presented in the book? What does this tell us about attitudes to class in the early twentieth century?

- In his preface, Buchan describes the novel as a 'shocker', which he defines as a book 'where the incidents defy the probabilities and march just inside the borders of the possible'. Do you think he succeeded with this last aim?

- How does the novel compare to more recent thrillers? How does Hannay differ from modern heroes?

BACKGROUND INFORMATION

- The novel has been filmed three times: in 1935, 1959 and 1978. The best known remains Alfred Hitchcock's 1935 version, which was ranked fourth in a British Film Institute poll of the greatest British films ever made.

- Like Jeffrey Archer and Edwina Currie, Buchan was a Conservative MP as well as a novelist.

- Buchan is said to have modelled the character of Richard Hannay partly on his friend Edmund Ironside, who worked as a spy in the Boer War.

- The adventures of Richard Hannay continue in four other novels – *Greenmantle* (1916), *Mr Standfast* (1919), *The Three Hostages* (1924) and *The Island of Sheep* (1936).

SUGGESTED COMPANION BOOKS

- *The Lord of the Rings* by J. R. R. TOLKIEN – some early sections of Tolkien's epic recall Buchan's pursuit narrative.

- *Casino Royale* by IAN FLEMING – suave secret agent James Bond takes over the derring-do where Richard Hannay left off.

- *The Third Man* by GRAHAM GREENE – twisting the espionage genre to explore moral and political anxieties.

- *The Da Vinci Code* by DAN BROWN – reviving the formula of conspiracies, ciphers, breathless pursuit and wrongly accused hero to blockbusting effect. But will future generations remember it as fondly as *The Thirty-Nine Steps*?

A Clockwork Orange

ANTHONY BURGESS

Published 1962 / Length 149 pages

*'We sat in the Korova Milkbar making up our rassoodocks
what to do with the evening . . .'*

The first thing the new reader of *A Clockwork Orange* notices is
its striking, idiosyncratic language. The novel is narrated by
Alex, a fifteen-year-old gang member, in 'Nadsat', which Burgess
created by combining words derived from Slavic and Russian
with Cockney rhyming slang. Although perplexing at first, this
impressively sustained voice soon becomes accessible. The narrative itself is set in a near-future dystopia, where teenage gangs
roam the streets committing acts of rape and 'ultra-violence'.
Alex initially boasts of his misdeeds, but his account soon shifts
to the attempts of the totalitarian state to rehabilitate him. As it
does so, the novel asks whether it's better to be forced to be good
than to choose to be bad. A quintessential cult novel, *A
Clockwork Orange* often divides book clubs into those who find
it too violent or obscure and those who are drawn in by its
unique inventiveness.

WHAT THE CRITICS SAID

'Burgess, a composer turned novelist, has an ebullient, musical
sense of language, and you pick up the meanings of the strange
words as the prose rhythms speed you along.' – PAULINE KAEL,
The New Yorker

DISCUSSION POINTS

- Why do you think Burgess chose to write the book in
  imaginary slang? What effect does it have on the novel's
  depiction of violence?

- At one point, the Prison Chaplain says, 'When a man cannot choose he ceases to be a man.' What is the novel saying about free will?

- Are there any parallels between today's 'hoodies' and the novel's 'droogs'? How does the current government's treatment of young offenders compare with that in the novel?
- The novel was once banned in some parts of the United States. Is it ever right to ban books?

BACKGROUND INFORMATION

- Stanley Kubrick's 1971 film adaptation was accused of inspiring several copycat attacks. However, it's a myth that the film was banned in the UK. In fact, Kubrick himself withdrew it from circulation after receiving threats to his safety.
- The novel's influence on popular culture has been immense, and many pop groups, including Heaven 17 and Moloko, have taken their names from it.
- Although *A Clockwork Orange* remains Burgess's most popular novel, the author himself regarded it as one of his lesser works.
- The experiments conducted on Alex parody the 'behavourist' work of psychologist B. F. Skinner.

SUGGESTED COMPANION BOOKS

- *Riddley Walker* by RUSSELL HOBAN – a post-apocalyptic novel written in an imaginary devolved English.
- *Brave New World* by ALDOUS HUXLEY (see page 114) – an earlier speculative fiction about the state's control of the individual.
- *Nineteen Eighty-Four* by GEORGE ORWELL (see page 158) – another linguistically inventive novel set in a grim future.
- *The Handmaid's Tale* by MARGARET ATWOOD (see page 20) – a novel about a state that subjugates women.

Top Ten British and American Classics

You may have noticed that these perennial favourites are missing an extended mention in *The Book Club Bible*. This is by no means a comment on their quality, but rather an expectation that readers may already have encountered these wonderful books – perhaps at school, perhaps on a published survey of the nation's most popular books – and discussed them with their book group. We urge you to reread them or discover them for the first time.

Pride and Prejudice by JANE AUSTEN

The Adventures of Augie March by SAUL BELLOW

Jane Eyre by CHARLOTTE BRONTË
(you may be interested to read *Wide Sargasso Sea*
by JEAN RHYS, which is something
of a 'prequel' to *Jane Eyre*)

Wuthering Heights by EMILY BRONTË
(you may be interested to read *Here on Earth*
by ALICE HOFFMAN, who was inspired by
the themes of *Wuthering Heights*)

Great Expectations by CHARLES DICKENS

Tess of the D'Urbervilles by THOMAS HARDY

A Thousand Acres by JANE SMILEY

The Grapes of Wrath by JOHN STEINBECK

Walden by HENRY DAVID THOREAU

The Age of Innocence by EDITH WHARTON

Top Ten World Classics

Dickens and Austen may be regular staples on the curriculum, but non-English-language books don't always receive such frequent billing or public exposure. Here is a necessarily limited snapshot of some world classics to tempt you and your book club into more exotic literary climes.

The House of the Spirits by ISABEL ALLENDE

The Master and Margarita by MIKHAIL BULGAKOV

The Outsider by ALBERT CAMUS

Chéri by COLETTE

The Leopard by GIUSEPPE TOMASI DI LAMPEDUSA

Crime and Punishment by FYODOR DOSTOEVSKY

Madame Bovary by GUSTAVE FLAUBERT

Miss Smilla's Feeling for Snow by PETER HØEG

Measuring The World by DANIEL KEHLMANN

My Name Is Red by ORHAN PAMUK

Oscar and Lucinda

Peter Carey

Published 1988 / Length 519 pages

Narrated by Oscar's great-grandson, *Oscar and Lucinda* tells the story of Oscar Hopkins, a delicate, English, flame-haired scarecrow of an Anglican reverend, and Lucinda Leplastrier, a fiercely independent and socially unschooled Australian heiress. Aged fifteen, Oscar makes a decision that changes his life course for ever, and ultimately sets him on a path to meet Lucinda, who suffers tribulations of her own at a young age, not the least of which is coming into an inheritance that immediately becomes a millstone around her neck. The book is set in the mid-nineteenth century, against a backdrop first of rural Hennacombe, Devon, and subsequently the spires of Oxford, smokestacks of London, drawing rooms of Sydney society and, finally, the inhospitable locales of the Australian outback. The book is a masterclass in character portraiture and Carey excels at detail throughout this intense, complex novel. While the action is sometimes slow-paced, the plot moves inexorably towards its calamitous conclusion, bolstered along the way by a passionate love story, intriguing psychological studies, dangerous addiction and fateful relationships.

Reader's opinion

'From the first page, you are assured by the author's skill that you are in safe hands. This book reminded me of a rich red wine: you cannot guzzle it down; each mouthful demands to be savoured. The dense detail in the book was impressive and evocative, though at times it made for a hard-going read, as there was just so much to take in.' – Kate, 26

Discussion points

● Consider the treatment of Oscar on the glassworks tour, as compared to Lucinda, and discuss. Would Lucinda's fate have differed had she been a man? Have things changed for businesswomen today?

● What does the passion for gambling represent? Why do you think Carey chose gambling as a metaphor?

● At times, the novel paints a bleak picture of life and the human character. Are there any redeeming factors?

● What view of religion does the book take? Are any of the characters truly moral?

● What, in your opinion, are Oscar and Lucinda's fatal flaws?

BACKGROUND INFORMATION

● *Oscar and Lucinda* won the 1988 Booker Prize and the 1989 Miles Franklin Award.

● Carey won the Booker Prize a second time in 2001, for *True History of the Kelly Gang*, a fictional exploration of the Ned Kelly story. Carey is one of only two writers to have won the prestigious award twice (the other is J. M. Coetzee).

● A film was made of the book in 1997, starring Ralph Fiennes as Oscar and Cate Blanchett as Lucinda.

SUGGESTED COMPANION BOOKS

● *Middlesex* by JEFFREY EUGENIDES (see page 66) – a sweeping family epic set against the backdrop of America and Asia Minor.

● *Father and Son* by EDMUND GOSSE – the autobiography of the English poet, by which Carey was partly inspired for *Oscar and Lucinda*.

● *Great Expectations* by CHARLES DICKENS – shifting social hierarchies and a memorable cast of characters; *The Spectator* described *Oscar and Lucinda* as having 'a Dickensian amplitude'.

Wise Children

Angela Carter

Published 1991 / Length 232 pages

'What a joy it is to dance and sing.'

Wise Children is a bawdy carnival of a novel narrated by Dora Chance, looking back over her ribald and sometimes ramshackle seventy-five years. Dora and her twin sister Nora are illegitimate offshoots of a sprawling theatrical dynasty, 'song-and-dance girls' who plied their trade on the stage – and once, ill-fatedly, on screen – throughout the twentieth century, having been born as the Zeppelins' bombs fell on London during the First World War. Carter explores themes of memory, paternity and legitimacy throughout: the Hazard clan is peppered with twins, disputed or dubious heredity, and multiple marriages of Shakespearean complexity. It's a joyous romp of a story, glittering with earthy humour and garlanded with a playful linguistic virtuosity. There are elements of magical realism to the plot, but such is the power of Dora's stardust-sprinkled tale, it is easy to suspend all disbelief and let it sweep you away, trailing paper moons, costume jewellery and greasepaint.

What the critics said

'Carter's insistent aim is to show how thoroughly the legitimate and illegitimate worlds are entangled, and in a country whose cultural life continues to be crippled by false distinction between "high" and "low", this is an important subject.' – *The Guardian*

Discussion points

● 'A father is a moveable feast': how does the novel explore the nature of paternity and, at times, incest? Are there any adequate fathers in the book?

- How well do you feel the roles of hazard, chance and coincidence are handled?
- What does the book communicate about memory and ageing – both gracefully and disgracefully?
- Who do you think is most likely to be the mother of Dora and Nora?
- How does Dora's narrative convey the changing face of London, and the world, over the course of the twentieth century?

BACKGROUND INFORMATION

- *Wise Children* was Angela Carter's eleventh and last novel, and this may inform its retrospective theme. It has also been suggested that she began writing it after having been diagnosed with cancer.
- Melchior and Peregrine have been seen as representative of the comic and tragic faces of theatre.
- In an interview about *Wise Children* in *New Writing* (1992), Angela Carter said: '[I wanted] to have a transparent prose that just ran, I wanted it to be very funny, and at the same time I wanted the complex ideas about paternity and the idea of Shakespeare as a cultural ideology.'

SUGGESTED COMPANION BOOKS

- *Nights at the Circus* by ANGELA CARTER – another earthy theatrical saga steeped in magical realism.
- *The Passion* by JEANETTE WINTERSON – gorgeous Venetian fantasy with fairy-tale elements.
- *A Midsummer Night's Dream, Hamlet, A Comedy of Errors* and *King Lear*, among others, by WILLIAM SHAKESPEARE – *Wise Children* includes numerous Shakespearean parallels.

2001: A Space Odyssey

Arthur C. Clarke

Published 1968 / Length 236 pages

2001: A Space Odyssey is the story of mankind's interaction with an unseen but super-intelligent race of alien beings. It shifts in time from the earliest origins of humanity to the near future, each part of the book revolving around a mysterious black monolith. In the beginning, the ape-like creature Moon-Gazer stumbles across the monolith. The monolith hypnotizes Moon-Gazer, and within days he has begun to use tools, to think for himself and to take the first steps on the road to civilization. When, millennia later, a similar monolith is discovered on the moon, an expedition is launched to try to discover where it came from, and the starship *Discovery*, piloted by the computer HAL 9000, sets forth on this mission. Soon, however, HAL begins to behave very strangely, and the only survivor of the original crew of five is Dave Bowman, a physicist. Bowman continues alone with the mission, until he reaches the moons of Saturn, where he gradually discovers that the people of the monolith still have plans for humanity . . .

WHAT THE CRITICS SAID

'*2001: A Space Odyssey* is one of the most important stories of all time. His Holiness sees no difference between what science is saying and what religion is saying.' – BILL BLAKEMORE, Vatican Correspondent for ABC, summarizing Pope John Paul II's reaction to the film of *2001*

DISCUSSION POINTS

● How well has the book aged since its 1968 publication? Clarke apparently assumed that by 2001 mankind would have established bases on the moon and achieved interplanetary travel, but that on the other hand the Cold War would still be going on. Do these inaccuracies affect our enjoyment of the story?

● What is the motivation of the monolith people? Are they performing experiments on mankind? If they wanted to help the human race, wasn't there an easier way to achieve this?

● Is *2001* fundamentally a story about evolution? Why do you think that the Pope was so keen on its message?

● How well do you think Clarke handles the descriptions of all the astonishing visual scenes in the book? How do these compare to Kubrick's vision, if you've also seen the film?

BACKGROUND INFORMATION

● The novel *2001: A Space Odyssey* was developed alongside the script for the film of the same name. Arthur C. Clarke and Stanley Kubrick worked on the idea together, based on two of Clarke's short stories, 'The Sentinel' and 'Encounter in the Dawn'.

● The 'perturbation manoeuvre' that takes *Discovery* past Jupiter was actually used by the *Voyager* spacecraft in 1979.

● The action in the film takes place on a moon of Jupiter rather than Saturn; this change was made because the MGM special-effects department couldn't produce convincing-looking rings.

SUGGESTED COMPANION BOOKS

● *2010: Odyssey Two* by ARTHUR C. CLARKE – what Professor Floyd and the Star-Child did next.

● *Last and First Men* by OLAF STAPLEDON – another, even more cosmic, interpretation of creation myths in a science-fiction context.

Jonathan Strange & Mr Norrell

SUSANNA CLARKE

Published 2004 / Length 1,024 pages

This epic novel (be sure that everyone in your book club is prepared to tackle such a doorstop!) is set in a fictitious nineteenth-century England. This England has a legacy of magic: myths of the Raven King, John Uskglass, permeate its consciousness, and its relationship with the supernatural realm of Fairie has only recently grown distant. However, English magic has fallen into disrepute and disuse. It is now the preserve of scholars, who study and annotate its history without ever actually practising it – until the enigmatic Mr Norrell emerges from his library and astounds the nation with his practical magical prowess. The book documents Norrell's adventures, his attempts to retain control of English magic, and his turbulent relationship with the other practical magician to emerge in this England: Jonathan Strange. Clarke beautifully portrays a fully realized fantasy world, with its own mythology, social mores and even literary canon (footnotes throughout refer to made-up works on English magic). Though unwieldy, this is a hugely satisfying read.

WHAT THE CRITICS SAID

'Forget media speculation about the huge advance and the Booker Prize longlisting: *Jonathan Strange & Mr Norrell* is not a book for cocktail gossip around a hip, urban table. It is a book for a favourite armchair, for readers in patched cardigans, with log fires and buttered muffins . . . This novel doesn't pretend to be as serious as the classics it admires, but it has an awful lot of fun dressing up as them.' – *The Daily Telegraph*

DISCUSSION POINTS

● In which genre do you think the novel belongs?

- The book has been seen as an allegory of the Industrial Revolution as, like magic, it unleashed potentially dangerous powers. How well does this interpretation hold up?
- How is the notion of 'Englishness' expressed throughout the novel?
- Did you find the book convincing about the properties and limitations of magic?
- Who narrates the book?

BACKGROUND INFORMATION

- The novel took ten years to write – Clarke says that she never knew whether it would ever be finished, let alone published.
- The author lists among her influences Jane Austen, C. S. Lewis (especially *The Magician's Nephew*), G. K. Chesterton's *The Man Who Was Thursday*, Umberto Eco's *The Name of the Rose*, and the TV series *Buffy the Vampire Slayer*.
- The confidence of publishers Bloomsbury in the book was such that the initial hardback print run was a staggering 250,000 copies.
- A film of the novel is currently in production by New Line Media.

SUGGESTED COMPANION BOOKS

- *The Earthsea Quartet* by URSULA K. LEGUIN – LeGuin's plausible magic was an influence on the book.
- *The Crimson Petal and the White* by MICHEL FABER – another satisfying epic set in the nineteenth century, though in a world without magic.
- *Sense and Sensibility* by JANE AUSTEN – compare the worlds of the genuine and 'mock' Regency novels. The title might also have suited *Jonathan Strange & Mr Norrell*.

What a Carve Up!

JONATHAN COE

Published 1994 / Length 512 pages

What a Carve Up! takes its reader on a spirited romp through the chequered family history of the well-to-do Winshaws. Beginning with the tragic death of RAF pilot Godfrey in the Second World War, it catalogues the ruthless ambitions of several family members who, by the 1980s, have been using their influence to devastating and damaging effect in the worlds of merchant banking, tabloid journalism and arms trading. Interspersed with the story of the power-hungry Winshaws are tales from the life of Michael Owen, a young writer commissioned to produce a biography of the Winshaw clan, though his attempts to get to the bottom of their many secrets are deliberately and continually blocked. Part detective story and part socio-political satire, and taking its title from the 1961 film comedy (which is revealed to have played a crucial role in Michael's formative years), *What a Carve Up!* is an unforgettably witty family saga filled with monstrous characters, insightful comment on the excesses of Thatcherite Britain, comic tragedy and countless unexpected twists and turns.

WHAT THE CRITICS SAID

'A big fat treat of a novel anatomizing the corrupt machinations of Britain's free-market power-brokers today – politicians, captains of industry, arms traders, media tycoons – with immense inventiveness and exuberant black humour.' – *The Scotsman*

DISCUSSION POINTS

● How much of the book is a polemic against the evils of capitalism associated with 1980s Britain?

- Does the author succeed in provoking sympathy in the reader for any members of the Winshaw family?

- How do you feel about the character of Michael Owen and his role as biographer, and the interspersed references to his own life popping up throughout the narrative?

- Do you think that Aunt Tabitha really is mad, or is her behaviour merely a reaction to the dark, underhand dealings of various family members over the years?

- Is the author successful in maintaining fluency throughout the book, despite the ever-fluctuating sequence of events?

BACKGROUND INFORMATION

- *What a Carve Up!* is Coe's fourth novel, and won the 1995 *Mail on Sunday*/John Llewellyn Rhys Prize and the French Prix du Meilleur Livre Étranger.

- Coe was a university student from the early to mid-1980s, and attended numerous CND rallies and demos opposing the Thatcher government.

- Coe wrote his first book aged eleven, and was writing novels by the age of fifteen.

SUGGESTED COMPANION BOOKS

- *The House of Sleep* by JONATHAN COE – his fifth novel is a tangled web of relationships, coincidences and sleep disorders, jumping back and forth between dreams and reality.

- *Behind the Scenes at the Museum* by KATE ATKINSON (see page 18) – a meandering, semi-tragic family history set over four generations.

- *The Pursuit of Love* by NANCY MITFORD – a hilarious story chronicling the trials and tribulations of a unique 1930s upper-class British family.

The Alchemist

PAULO COELHO

Published 1988 / Length 192 pages

A fable mixed with esoteric but accessible messages, such as finding one's purpose in life, taking control of one's destiny and making dreams a reality, *The Alchemist* follows the journey of Santiago, a young Spanish shepherd boy, who yearns to leave his books and sheep behind for a life of freedom and travel. Santiago's recurring dream about buried treasure at the Pyramids, and an encounter with the mysterious King of Salem, prompt him to take action and follow his dream, which ultimately brings about profound transformations. Santiago's journey transports the reader from Spain to northern Africa, yet not at any particular point in time, giving the story a universal, timeless appeal.

READER'S OPINION

'It is a well-told little story and easy to digest. If it encourages more people to read, then that's very positive. However, I found the book too sentimental for my taste, repetitive and as subtle as a sledgehammer.' – STAN, 34

DISCUSSION POINTS

● Fables form part of an ancient tradition of storytelling and have the purpose of teaching the reader a lesson or imparting advice. What messages did you take from the book, if any? Do you think *The Alchemist* is a successful fable?

● Santiago's father tries to discourage his son from travelling and says there really is no place like home. 'They come in search of new things, but when they leave they are basically the same people they were when they arrived.' Do you think travel is a transformative experience?

- The Englishman is searching for 'a universal language, understood by everybody'. What do you think that language is? Do you think he has been looking in the right places?
- Do you agree with the King of Salem that 'the world's greatest lie is that humans have no free will'?

BACKGROUND INFORMATION

- *The Alchemist* is one of the bestselling books in history, selling over 40 million copies in more than 150 countries.
- *The Alchemist* took Coelho fifteen days to write.
- In 1986 (two years before writing *The Alchemist*), Paulo Coelho walked the Road of Santiago, an ancient Spanish pilgrimage.

SUGGESTED COMPANION BOOKS

- *Animal Farm* by GEORGE ORWELL – the classic allegory, which satirizes communism.
- *The Little Prince* by ANTOINE DE SAINT-EXUPÉRY – a children's book about a young prince, who also leaves his home in search of his dreams.
- *Jonathan Livingston Seagull* by RICHARD BACH – a fable about a young seagull learning to fly, preaching messages about non-conformity and self-sacrifice.
- *Siddhartha* by HERMANN HESSE – another quest for enlightenment, with parallels to *The Alchemist*.

The Woman in White

WILKIE COLLINS

Published 1860 / Length 720 pages

'This is a story of what a woman's patience can endure.'

The Woman in White is an intriguing and mystifying story of stolen identities, corruption, deceit, money and social anxiety. Soon after Walter Hartright helps a mysterious woman, dressed all in white, on a dark road in the middle of the night, he is disturbed to learn that she may have escaped from an asylum. Following this encounter, Hartright gains the position of art teacher at Limmeridge House, home to half-sisters Laura Fairlie and Marian Halcombe. He soon falls madly in love with the younger sister, Laura, despite the fact that she is already betrothed to Sir Percival Glyde, whom she does not love. When Hartright discovers that the woman in white could be linked to the lives of these young women, he finds himself caught up in a race against time to prevent a disastrous plot from unfolding.

WHAT THE CRITICS SAID

'Wilkie Collins tried to rid *The Woman in White* of "blemishes". He succeeded. You can call it fantastical and full of coincidences, but it is hard to argue that the plotting is flawed.' – *The Times*

DISCUSSION POINTS

- 'Having helped her to avoid recapture, he [Hartright] is racked with guilt that he has let loose that uncaged femininity that is the duty of every respectable man to control' – Lynne Pickett, *The Sensation Novel* (1996). How does *The Woman in White* tackle the issue of gender and power?

- Sensation fiction is concerned with social anxiety. How does the novel approach the theme of class?

- Do you think the use of different narrators by Collins is effective? Did you trust all the narrators?

BACKGROUND INFORMATION

- *The Woman in White* has been classed as sensation fiction as it aims to appeal to readers' nerves as opposed to their reason. During the nineteenth century, sensation fiction was seen to be an effeminate form of writing because it was usually concerned with the psychological in a domestic setting, as opposed to the supernatural.

- *The Woman in White* was originally published in serial form in Charles Dickens's magazine, *All Year Round*.

- Collins claimed that he was the first author of fiction to use the narratives of different characters as the central structure of a novel.

- In 2004, *The Woman in White* was made into a West End musical by composer Andrew Lloyd Webber.

SUGGESTED COMPANION BOOKS

- *Lady Audley's Secret* by MARY BRADDON – corresponding themes of deceit and corruption. Both have a similar detective style.

- *The Law and the Lady* by WILKIE COLLINS – comparable narrative styles with regards to each character knowing separate pieces of the puzzle.

- *Sense and Sensibility* by JANE AUSTEN – explores the special relationship between sisters.

- *Tess of the D'Urbervilles* by THOMAS HARDY – another example of sensation fiction, in which the plot affects the reader's nerves.

Heart of Darkness

Joseph Conrad

Published 1902 / Length 112 pages

Aboard a ship anchored in the Thames, a sailor called Marlow tells of his journey up the Congo River in search of an ivory trader named Kurtz. As he travels deeper into Africa, Marlow becomes increasingly obsessed with Kurtz, who has apparently established himself as a god figure among the natives. The 'darkness' of the title seems to fall across every passage of the novel. Environments and people are described as 'dark' or 'gloomy', or are not described at all: Marlow's account frequently stutters with words like 'unspeakable' and 'inconceivable'. Yet through this foggy and ambiguous narrative, Conrad hints at the failures of imperialism and the savagery that's unleashed when the façade of civilization breaks down – notions that must truly have been 'unspeakable' to some contemporary readers.

Heart of Darkness is a short novel that casts a large and suitably murky shadow across modern fiction. Written at the very end of the nineteenth century (though published in 1902), it touches upon themes that would dominate the literature of the following one.

READER'S OPINION

'I thought it was a brilliant novel, which presented some very bleak notions about the human condition. It left me feeling depressed and hollow, but it's one of those books that really stays with you.' – STUART, 32

DISCUSSION POINTS

● How does Marlow's mental state affect his depiction of the environments through which he travels?

- Who is the book's most important character – Marlow or Kurtz?
- Why do you think Conrad chose to have Marlow relating the tale to the anonymous narrator, rather than directly to the reader?
- In 1975, Nigerian writer Chinua Achebe accused the book of racism, on the grounds that it portrayed Africans as an extension of the dangerous jungle. Was he right to do so?

BACKGROUND INFORMATION

- Francis Ford Coppola's classic film *Apocalypse Now* (1979) transposed the characters and events of *Heart of Darkness* to the Vietnam War.
- Despite his reputation as one of the giants of English literature, Conrad was born in the Polish Ukraine and didn't learn English until he was twenty-one.
- The novel was inspired by Conrad's experience of captaining a steamboat up the Congo in 1889.

SUGGESTED COMPANION BOOKS

- *Things Fall Apart* by CHINUA ACHEBE (see page 10) – giving voice to the inhabitants of the 'dark continent', this novel can be read as a post-colonial response to *Heart of Darkness*.
- *Lord of the Flies* by WILLIAM GOLDING (see page 84) – subverting the adventure yarn to depict the fragility of civilization.
- *The Strange Case of Dr Jekyll and Mr Hyde* by ROBERT LOUIS STEVENSON – another short novel exposing the savage impulses beneath the composed veneer of Victorian society.
- *The Waste Land* by T. S. ELIOT – this famous long poem deals with the same weighty themes as Conrad's book; Eliot used a quotation from the latter as an epigraph in an early draft.

Captain Corelli's Mandolin

LOUIS DE BERNIÈRES

Published 1994 / Length 435 pages

Captain Corelli's Mandolin has become a modern classic, and deservedly so. Louis de Bernières's tale is of a beautiful Greek girl, Pelagia, from the tiny island of Cephalonia, and her passionate love for Captain Antonio Corelli, a visiting soldier from the lightly occupying Italian Army, during the Second World War. The book is also an attempt to define and describe music in words, as the notes and harmonies of Antonio's mandolin weave around Pelagia and her world. But tragedy is never far away in wartime, and soon Cephalonia's rural harmony is shattered by the arrival of the brutal Germans, whose actions suddenly and unexpectedly fill the pages of the novel with blood. The plot twists and winds its way from the old ways of rural Greece to the new, and so we see those things that change with the mere effort of politicians – such as the coming of electricity; those that take more effort of will – such as changes in attitudes; and that which struggles to remain the same despite the passage of time: love.

READER'S OPINION

'Louis de Bernières has an incredible way of describing the personal – he is intensely intimate and his superb portrayal of characters spans generations. It is as though they are living parallel lives across time and you are actually participating in those lives. In *Captain Corelli's Mandolin*, he creates two vibrant descriptions of two entirely different worlds – the national events surrounding the Second World War in which Cephalonia is merely a pawn, and the personal events of his characters. Yet the two are so interwoven that you are not conscious of them being separate at all – it is more that one is a reflection of the other.' – GISÈLE, 32

DISCUSSION POINTS

- Some readers find that there is a central inconsistency to the plot when Antonio acts out of character, which makes the remaining narrative unconvincing. Do you agree with this? If not, is it because the story continues to sweep you away, or for some different reason?

- How well do you feel the author manages to fuse descriptions of music with the narrative?

- The novel is written from the perspective of several different characters. Did any of these voices jar with you, or are they all equally successful?

BACKGROUND INFORMATION

- *Captain Corelli's Mandolin* won the 1995 Commonwealth Writers' Prize for Best Book.

- The book was made into a successful film in 2001 starring Nicholas Cage and Penélope Cruz.

SUGGESTED COMPANION BOOKS

- *The Hundred Secret Senses* by AMY TAM – another tale of hidden secrets and ghostly appearances.

- *The House of the Spirits* by ISABEL ALLENDE – several generations in a foreign land are vividly conjured.

- *Birdsong* by SEBASTIAN FAULKS (see page 70) – another modern classic that examines love against a backdrop of political conflict, this time set during the First World War.

The Inheritance of Loss

Kiran Desai

Published 2006 / Length 324 pages

The triple locations of Desai's book – the Himalayas in north-eastern India; New York; and Cambridge, England – reflect the multiple inheritances of contemporary Indians in a globalized, post-imperial world. Querying and gentle, but insistent in tone, *The Inheritance of Loss* examines the impact of economic subordination and the notion of cultural inferiority during and after the days of empire. Desai unearths the roots of British-educated judge Jemubhai's rejection of his Indian heritage, exploring his self-loathing as he tries desperately to win approval, while fearing that he is inescapably different from the Westerners he would like to mimic.

Structured in snippets, the book could seem frustratingly episodic, but each little section contains a flash of revelation. Across the vast historical sweep of the book, Desai weaves a delicate, loose-knit tapestry of immense narrative scope, tugging together the strands. Quietly, determinedly, like the mist that seeps into and chills the tumbledown house on the hillside, the story insinuates its way into your imagination. Yet its reflections on hatred and humiliation remain ruthlessly exact.

WHAT THE CRITICS SAID

'[S]he describes the lives of people fated to experience modern life as a continuous affront to their notions of order, dignity and justice.' – *The New York Times*

DISCUSSION POINTS

● The judge's house is disintegrating – but is the 'old order' passing, or do new political relationships in our globalized world reproduce old patterns of domination?

- Consider the evolution of Gyan and Sai's relationship. Why does the eventual outcome occur? Where do Gyan's humiliation and hate spring from?
- Seeing the judge's solitude as a student at Cambridge helps to explain some of his later behaviour, but does it excuse it?
- Does Sai offer hope for a better future?

BACKGROUND INFORMATION

- When *The Inheritance of Loss* won the Booker Prize in 2007, Desai was thirty-five – the youngest ever woman to take home the coveted award.
- Desai's mother, Anita Desai, has been nominated for the Booker Prize three times, but has never won. As she accepted the £50,000 reward, Kiran declared: 'To my mother I owe a debt so profound and so great that this book feels as much hers as it does mine.'

SUGGESTED COMPANION BOOKS

- *Dr Zhivago* by BORIS PASTERNAK – a wonderfully evocative epic; a tale of the coming and passing of first love soured by the intrusion of political turmoil.
- *Rebecca* by DAPHNE DU MAURIER and *Beloved* by TONI MORRISON (see pages 60 and 142, respectively) – both novels are set in atmospheric houses saturated with history.
- *Brideshead Revisited* by EVELYN WAUGH (see page 216) – the same wistful, elegiac tone, though Waugh's vision of a lost past is more idealized.

House of Sand and Fog

Andre Dubus III

Published 1999 / Length 365 pages

*'The county has petitioned the court in its behalf, Mrs Lazaro.
This should come as no surprise to you. I'm sure you had ample
warning; your house is up for auction starting tomorrow morning.'*

When Kathy Nicolo is evicted from her house following a case of
mistaken identity, it comes as the last straw. Having struggled to
recover from cocaine addiction, she has recently been abandoned
by her husband for another woman; the house her father
bequeathed to her was the one stable thing in her life. Before she's
able to prove the county's error, however, the property is sold at
auction to Massoud Amir Behrani, a former colonel in the
Iranian Air Force, and she finds herself caught in a legal loophole.
Behrani, meanwhile, has pinned all his hopes, and finances, on
his new property, and he vows not to relinquish this final chance
to restore his family to wealth, status and security. For both Kathy
and Behrani, the house on Bisgrove Street becomes the key to
their future happiness, as the repercussions of a clerical error
spiral out of control.

What the critics said

'The most rending kind of war is not between two hatreds, but
between two hopes. Dubus sets out the growing confrontation
with chilly ingenuity and a remarkably observant compassion.
A fine and prophetic novel.' – *Los Angeles Times*

Discussion points

- Why do you think Kathy is so strongly attracted to Lester?
  Is their relationship a destructive one?
- 'What is it I have done except provide for my family?' To
  what extent do you agree with Behrani's convictions?

- Does racism affect the ways in which the characters interact with each other? What is the author saying about the challenges of immigration?
- Much has been made of the ending of the book. Do you feel that it reaches a satisfying conclusion? Could the author have ended it at a different point?

BACKGROUND INFORMATION

- In 2003, the book was filmed by Ukrainian-American director Vadim Perelman, starring Ben Kingsley as Behrani and Jennifer Connelly as Kathy. It was nominated for three Academy Awards, including Best Actor for Ben Kingsley.
- Andre Dubus III's father, Andre Dubus, was a recognized author in his own right, and published nine collections of short fiction and a novel during his lifetime.
- *House of Sand and Fog* was shortlisted for the National Book Award 1999 and the IMPAC Literary Award 2001. It was also selected for Oprah's Book Club.

SUGGESTED COMPANION BOOKS

- *Cathedral* by RAYMOND CARVER – short stories about suburban America, with recurring themes of addiction and recovery.
- *The Namesake* by JHUMPA LAHIRI – immigrants trying to settle in America; conflicting cultures.
- *Black Cherry Blues* by JAMES LEE BURKE – tackling addiction in extreme circumstances.

Rebecca

Daphne du Maurier

Published 1938 / Length 448 pages

A year after Maxim de Winter's first wife, Rebecca, is drowned off the coast near to his mansion, Manderley, he remarries. Maxim meets his new bride while travelling abroad; she is an innocent, reserved young woman who remains unnamed throughout the novel, and whose fate it is to relate the story. Living in the shadow of Maxim's first wife, the narrator's life becomes consumed by Rebecca's memory, a state of affairs largely encouraged by the malignant and cruel housekeeper, Mrs Danvers. For much of the novel, Rebecca seems to overpower the heroine, as her name echoes throughout the house, destroying all efforts the narrator makes to become its mistress. However, all is not what it seems at Manderley and, as the plot unfolds, the seemingly perfect appearance of the house and its grounds belies a multitude of secrets. It soon becomes evident that deceit and corruption are central to the novel's denouement.

READER'S OPINION

'A riveting and intense read, *Rebecca* is a wonderful novel, full of mystery and intrigue. The memory of Rebecca is as strong, if not stronger, than all the other living characters, making the book a chilling read. I highly recommend it.' – NICKY, 22

DISCUSSION POINTS

● 'Last night I dreamt I went to Manderley again.' The book's opening sentence suggests that the narrator uses the novel to look back at past events. How effective do you think this technique is, and why do you think the story is told in this way?

- Do we feel a connection with the narrator, or are we drawn more to Rebecca? For whom does the reader ultimately feel more sorry? Do you think the plot of the book relies on the narrator being nameless?
- How are the grounds of Manderley significant in setting the scene in which the events unfold?
- How does du Maurier make Rebecca's presence so forceful? What role does Mrs Danvers play in this? Is Rebecca's character reflected in the housekeeper?
- What do you think the book's message is regarding the role of women in a patriarchal society?

BACKGROUND INFORMATION

- Classed as a gothic romance, *Rebecca* is Daphne du Maurier's most famous novel. She modelled the book on Charlotte Brontë's *Jane Eyre,* drawing parallels between Jane and the nameless heroine in *Rebecca.*
- Manderley was based on du Maurier's own house in Cornwall.
- *Rebecca* was made into a film by Alfred Hitchcock in 1940, winning two Oscars and nominations for nine other awards.
- Daphne du Maurier was cousin to the Llewelyn Davies boys, on whom J. M. Barrie based his famous work, *Peter Pan.*

SUGGESTED COMPANION BOOKS

- *Desperate Remedies* by THOMAS HARDY – deals with the themes of wives, deception and 'the other woman'.
- *Uncle Silas* by JOSEPH SHERIDAN LE FANU – compare the characters of the housekeepers, Mrs Danvers and Madame de la Rougierre.
- *Jane Eyre* by CHARLOTTE BRONTË – consider similarities and differences in narrative, character and plot.

A Spell of Winter

Helen Dunmore

Published 1995 / Length 313 pages

A Spell of Winter is set during the early years of the twentieth century and explores the complex relationship between a brother and sister. Catherine and Rob Allen have been left parentless. Their mother went abroad early in their childhood, while their father slipped away from them into madness and a premature death. Ostensibly under the care of their grandfather in his decaying country house, the children are looked after by the ever-dependable maidservant Kate and their governess, Miss Gallagher, whose open disapproval of Rob and overly possessive affection for Catherine lead the children to dislike her intensely. Surrounded by a wall of silence about the past, and with Kate and Miss Gallagher locked in opposition with regard to their welfare, the children's only certainty in this oppressive atmosphere is their love for one another. Yet at what point does love turn bad? As Cathy begins to be courted by her grandfather's neighbour, the wealthy but middle-aged Mr Bullivant, and Rob starts to pursue the beautiful Livvy, their need to hold on to each other intensifies. The outside world closes in, and the consequences of their devotion become shameful and horrifying.

WHAT THE CRITICS SAID

'An intensely gripping book . . . written so seductively that some passages sing out from the page, like music for the eyes.' – *The Sunday Times*

DISCUSSION POINTS

- *A Spell of Winter* is often categorized as a gothic novel. Discuss the characteristics that make it so.

- 'We were barred and left outside to swallow whatever story we were given.' How are Rob and Catherine affected by the secrecy that surrounds them?

- '[R]oses are the queens of the summer, aren't they, Catherine?' Why does Catherine reply that she does not like roses? Discuss the use of flower and plant motifs throughout the book.

- 'Did other people have this insane drive to destroy what was best for them, and cherish what was worst? Was that what our father had given us?' Discuss the portrayal of the various parents in the novel.

- Is it true to say that the gathering momentum of the First World War externalizes the conflict that is taking place in the lives of Catherine and Rob?

BACKGROUND INFORMATION

- *A Spell of Winter* won the first Orange Prize for Fiction in 1996.

SUGGESTED COMPANION BOOKS

- *Shadow Baby* by MARGARET FORSTER – a compelling story that examines the mother–daughter relationship over several generations.

- *The Cement Garden* by IAN MCEWAN – concerns a family of abandoned children adapting to life without their parents, and their subverted childhood.

- *Jane Eyre* by CHARLOTTE BRONTË and *The Turn of the Screw* by HENRY JAMES (see page 122) – corresponding characters of orphaned children and sinister carers, combined with classic gothic elements.

- *Hatter's Castle* by A. J. CRONIN – a young woman seeks comfort in the arms of her lover, and is forced to keep the consequences a secret from her tyrannical father.

Top Ten Quick Reads

In our jam-packed lives, it can sometimes be a struggle to find the time to read the latest book club choice. So here are ten quality short reads – some of barely 200 pages, others with a lightning-quick pace – to help you out during those busy weeks when ploughing through a 600-page epic just isn't realistic. After all, the best things come in small packages.

Untouchable by MULK RAJ ANAND

An Awfully Big Adventure by BERYL BAINBRIDGE

A Month in the Country by J. L. CARR

The God Boy by IAN CROSS

The Barrytown Trilogy by RODDY DOYLE
(three quick reads in one)

The Bookshop by PENELOPE FITZGERALD

Metamorphosis by FRANZ KAFKA

Moon Tiger by PENELOPE LIVELY

Bonjour Tristesse by FRANÇOISE SAGAN

The Prime of Miss Jean Brodie by MURIEL SPARK

Top Ten Challenging Reads

Got to grips with *We Need to Talk About Kevin*? Discussed to death the many cultural resonances in *Midnight's Children*? Weary of dissecting Woolf? Then why not try your hand at these challenging reads? They're all wonderful, highly acclaimed books – but it may take a bit more effort and elbow grease to get the most out of them.

Possession by A. S. BYATT

The Name of the Rose by UMBERTO ECO

Ulysses by JAMES JOYCE

The Poisonwood Bible by BARBARA KINGSOLVER

The Unbearable Lightness of Being by MILAN KUNDERA

Dr Zhivago by BORIS PASTERNAK

How the Dead Live by WILL SELF

A Suitable Boy by VIKRAM SETH

Anna Karenina by LEO TOLSTOY

Germinal by ÉMILE ZOLA

Middlesex

JEFFREY EUGENIDES

Published 2002 / Length 529 pages

*'I was born twice: first, as a baby girl, on a remarkably smogless
Detroit day in January of 1960; and then again, as a teenage boy,
in an emergency room near Petoskey, Michigan, in August of 1974.'*

So begins *Middlesex*, a lush, engaging and epic story that follows the
Stephanides family from war-torn Asia Minor in 1922, through
Detroit during the sixties race riots, to present-day Berlin. Narrated
by hermaphrodite teenager Cal (previously Calliope), a third-
generation Stephanides, it covers many events that define the
twentieth century – Prohibition, immigration, race clashes, the
Nation of Islam – but always comes back to the twists and turns of
daily life. A truly multicultural novel, the book attempts to deal
with the melting pot of modern life; how past and present are
entwined with the family's joint American and Greek heritage. The
Stephanideses' changing fortunes throughout the century echo
America's evolving sense of self, while Cal's adolescent uncertainties
come to symbolize much more: the nature of identity, whether
personal or national.

WHAT THE CRITICS SAID

'[An] uproarious epic, at once funny and sad . . . Mr Eugenides
has a keen sociological eye for twentieth-century American life
. . . But it's his emotional wisdom, his nuanced insight into his
characters' inner lives, that lends this book its cumulative
power.' – *The New York Times*

DISCUSSION POINTS

● The novel frequently skips between time periods, and
  withholds information. Is Cal/Calliope a reliable narrator?
  How can he/she know so much about the past?

- Discuss the clash in the novel between traditional storytelling techniques and Cal/Calliope's moments of postmodernism.
- Mount Olympus is the original home of the principal gods of the Greek pantheon. What roles do fate and classical mythology play in the novel? Does *Middlesex* suggest that some things are destined to occur?

BACKGROUND INFORMATION

- *Middlesex* won the 2003 Pulitzer Prize in Fiction and was selected for Oprah's Book Club in 2007.
- The novel is only Eugenides's second book, after *The Virgin Suicides*, which was made into a film in 1999 starring Kirsten Dunst.
- *Middlesex* took almost ten years to write, and was originally planned as a much shorter piece.
- The Stephanideses' heritage is informed by the author's own background; the Eugenideses are also Greeks from Asia Minor.

SUGGESTED COMPANION BOOKS

- *Geek Love* by KATHERINE DUNN – a family with varying genetic anomalies have to cope with daily life after their circus disbands.
- *Nights at the Circus* by ANGELA CARTER – stars half-bird, half-woman, Fevvers, and is set in London and Eastern Europe in the early twentieth century.
- *The Corrections* by JONATHAN FRANZEN (see page 76) – another epic novel that asks how much our identity is defined by our family.
- *Orlando* by VIRGINIA WOOLF – another 'hermaphrodite' narrator takes charge in this playful and experimental novel.

As I Lay Dying

WILLIAM FAULKNER

Published 1935 / Length 248 pages

A portrait of life in the American Deep South, *As I Lay Dying* tells the story of the Bundren family as they embark on a journey to bury their mother in her home town of Jefferson, Mississippi. Written as a stream of consciousness, the book's chapters are variously narrated by several characters, each with a distinctive style to reflect their unique personality, right down to their dialect. A depiction of a family learning to work together to overcome obstacles, the novel is more strikingly a collection of personal journeys, as each family member finds their own way to come to terms with grief. Laced with black humour, Faulkner's tale is at times grotesque, and yet also filled with heart, as we witness the Bundrens' battles and triumphs.

READER'S OPINION

'At first glance this book seems challenging, but once you grasp the narrative style, the characters' personal stories become absorbing, Faulkner's style fascinating, and the Bundrens' heroic struggles against adversity win you over.' – SALLY, 22

DISCUSSION POINTS

- Faulkner's representations of human thought processes are often incredibly poetic, especially in the case of Darl. How realistic do you find the narrative? Is Faulkner right to take some artistic licence?

- The Bundrens are not really presented in a positive light, either as a family or individuals, yet their mission is honourable. Ultimately, could their journey be interpreted as heroic, with Anse as the villain?

- Darl's narrative dominates the book. What does this say

about him and the other characters? What disparate character traits do we become aware of through the different narrative voices? How does Faulkner achieve this?

- Though Addie narrates only one chapter of the book, she could be seen as its centre. How are issues of motherhood and family presented? Are the Bundrens traditional?

BACKGROUND INFORMATION

- William Faulkner grew up in Oxford, Mississippi, on which Jefferson in the fictional county Yoknapatawpha is based. The population was made up of poor farmers like the Bundrens, who scraped a living from the land.

- The title *As I Lay Dying* is a line from Homer's *The Odyssey*; the link to the epic genre suggests that Faulkner's book is a mock epic. It elevates the journey of a poor, small-town family into a quest for greatness.

- Faulkner wrote the book in six weeks while working in a university boiler room, shovelling coal to pay the mortgage. Later in his life Faulkner became famous, moving to Hollywood to become a scriptwriter.

SUGGESTED COMPANION BOOKS

- *The Adventures of Huckleberry Finn* by MARK TWAIN (see page 208) – like Faulkner's, Twain's book is a celebration of the South.

- *The Grapes of Wrath* by JOHN STEINBECK – focuses on a poor family forced to make a journey and their developing relationships.

- *On the Road* by JACK KEROUAC – similarly experimental and written in stream-of-consciousness style, detailing the travels of friends across America.

Birdsong

SEBASTIAN FAULKS

Published 1993 / Length 503 pages

Packed with period detail and enlivened by an erotically charged romance, *Birdsong* has already become one of the classic depictions of the First World War. Stephen Wraysford, a junior partner in a textiles firm, is sent to Amiens in 1910 to study production techniques. While there, he begins a passionate affair with Isabelle Azaire, the wife of his host, and they elope together. Six years later, Stephen returns to France as a lieutenant in the British Army. He enters the trenches at the Somme, where he endures the privations, military offensives and enemy counter-attacks that form part of everyday life there. In the trenches we also encounter Captain Michael Weir, Wraysford's friend, and Jack Firebrace, a former miner employed to dig beneath enemy lines. Wraysford's story is interspersed with that of his granddaughter, Elizabeth Benson, who experiences a similarly troubled romance, and Faulks draws parallels between the two pairs of lovers.

READER'S OPINION

'What stayed in my mind was the incredibly in-depth description of life in the trenches. Although I knew of the conditions, this is the first book that really brought home to me all the horror and filth of the trenches – the "reality" of the time.' – LINDY, 40

DISCUSSION POINTS

- What do you think Faulks is trying to achieve with the character of Jack Firebrace? How does Firebrace's experience of the war differ from Wraysford's?

- Stephen Wraysford often seems emotionally detached from what happens around him. Is this a fair assessment? How is he affected by what he witnesses in the trenches?

- In what ways do the sections of the novel set in the 1970s add to the overall effect? How would the novel change if they were removed?
- Has reading this novel changed your perspective of the First World War? How does it differ from other depictions of wartime?

BACKGROUND INFORMATION

- *Birdsong* is the second volume in Faulks's unofficial 'French trilogy'; the first volume is *The Girl at the Lion d'Or* (1989), while *Charlotte Gray* (1998) completes the trilogy.
- Faulks wrote *Birdsong* in under six months, researching and writing it simultaneously.
- The book came thirteenth in the BBC's 'The Big Read', a campaign to discover Britain's most popular novels.

SUGGESTED COMPANION BOOKS

- *Regeneration* by PAT BARKER – another modern perspective on the First World War.
- *All Quiet on the Western Front* by ERICH MARIA REMARQUE – the trenches from a German soldier's perspective; possibly the most famous novel of the First World War.
- *Captain Corelli's Mandolin* by LOUIS DE BERNIÈRES (see page 54) – love and loss in wartime.
- *Jarhead* by ANTHONY SWOFFORD – this Gulf War memoir provides a comparison with modern warfare.

The Great Gatsby

F. Scott Fitzgerald

Published 1926 / Length 188 pages

The Great Gatsby is arguably the greatest American novel ever written. Jay Gatsby is an enigmatic millionaire who lives in a grand villa on Long Island Sound, across the bay from Nick Carraway, the narrator, and from Tom and Daisy Buchanan. Gatsby is obsessed with Daisy, his childhood sweetheart, who is also Nick's cousin. With Nick's help, Gatsby meets Daisy and the two begin an affair, as the summer turns into a round of opulent parties at Gatsby's house. Although Tom is also having an affair, he becomes jealous and begins to spread word that Gatsby is a bootlegger and a criminal. Emotions heighten, cars crash and wrong assumptions are made, ending, as we discover very early on in the book, with Gatsby dead. Nick is the only person who attends his funeral: all the partygoers, even his criminal accomplices, have abandoned him. It is a novel of fine observations and fabulous flourishes, such as its famous final sentence.

WHAT THE CRITICS SAID

'Reading it now for the seventh or eighth time, I am more convinced than ever not merely that it is Fitzgerald's masterwork, but that it is *the* American masterwork, the finest work of fiction by any of this country's writers.' – *The Washington Post*

DISCUSSION POINTS

- 'So we beat on, boats against the current . . .' *The Great Gatsby* has one of the most famous last sentences in literature. How does it sum up the themes of the book?

- By the end of the novel, Nick Carraway is thoroughly disgusted with Tom and Daisy. Do you agree with this opinion? Is Nick really in a position to judge them?

- How many real-life Great Gatsbys can you think of? Did Robert Maxwell have something of Gatsby about him, for example?
- What is it about Gatsby that people don't like? It can hardly be his occupation as a bootlegger, as all the other characters drink alcohol.

BACKGROUND INFORMATION

- F. Scott Fitzgerald is widely credited with having first coined the phrase which named the era of 1920s America as 'the jazz age'.
- *The Great Gatsby* has been filmed four times, most famously in 1974 by Jack Clayton, with a screenplay by Francis Ford Coppola. Truman Capote wrote the original screenplay for this production, but it was never filmed; it suggested that Nick and Gatsby were gay.
- An American edition of *The Great Gatsby* has a famous painting by Francis Cugat on the cover, which was completed before the novel was finished and 'written into the novel', according to Fitzgerald.

SUGGESTED COMPANION BOOKS

- *Tender Is the Night* by F. SCOTT FITZGERALD – another classic and much-filmed story of doomed love among the wealthy.
- *Vile Bodies* by EVELYN WAUGH – once again we are among the rich young things of the 1920s and 1930s.
- *Twilight Sleep* by EDITH WHARTON – explores the glittering New York scene of the 1920s and its effects on its key players.

A Room with a View

E. M. FORSTER

Published 1908 / Length 256 pages

The novel opens in Edwardian Italy, where Lucy Honeychurch and her spinster cousin, Charlotte Bartlett, are lodged in a hotel in Florence. The trip is Lucy's first abroad and she is keen to expand her narrow experiences by seeing the real Italy. In reality, she encounters a delightful cast of English tourists, including the Emersons, a liberal father and son; the astutely observant Mr Beebe; and intrepid lady novelist Miss Lavish. All of these characters influence Lucy in different ways as she starts to question who she is and what she wants. The second half of the book is based at the Honeychurch home back in England, where the same characters reappear and Lucy is thrown into increasing turmoil, as she is forced to decide whether to follow her heart or her head. Will love conquer all?

Although essentially a coming-of-age story, the most enduring charm of *A Room with a View* is the wry social commentary of Forster's narration. Beautifully written and constructed, it is an exceedingly funny book filled with subtle ironies and keen observations.

READER'S OPINION

'A wonderful social comedy, which has everything: Brits abroad, love, break-ups, families and religion. A glorious read, and the reason I moved to Italy!' – CATHRYN, 34

DISCUSSION POINTS

- What is the symbolic significance of the room and the view? Which characters do you think embody these different outlooks on life?
- Do you think it is a happy ending? Does Lucy make the right decision?

- How does Lucy change throughout the book? Does anyone else in the novel develop, or do the other characters stay constant?
- Critics, including Forster himself, have called the book 'thin'; however, it is widely regarded as Forster's most popular and readable book. What do you think?

BACKGROUND INFORMATION

- The book took Forster over six years to complete, during which time he also wrote *Where Angels Fear to Tread* and *The Longest Journey*.
- Forster wrote a sequel, *A View without a Room*, which was published in July 1958 in *The Observer* and *The New York Times*. It updates the reader on what has happened to the characters in the fifty years since we left them. It was included in the 1978 Penguin edition of *A Room with a View*, but is otherwise largely unavailable in book form.
- In 1986, *A Room with a View* was made into a successful film by Merchant Ivory Productions. The movie won three Academy Awards, including Best Screenplay for its adaptation from the original novel.

SUGGESTED COMPANION BOOKS

- *Rebecca* by DAPHNE DU MAURIER (see page 60) – the transformation of a young, naive girl as she discovers more about those she loves, and herself.
- *I Capture the Castle* by DODIE SMITH – a coming-of-age romance set against a backdrop of an eccentric family.
- *Miss Garnet's Angel* by SALLEY VICKERS – think Charlotte Bartlett travelling to Italy alone.
- *Mansfield Park* by JANE AUSTEN – a hugely enjoyable wry social satire.

The Corrections

JONATHAN FRANZEN

Published 2001 / Length 568 pages

The Corrections was launched with a blaze of publicity in September 2001 as the new great American novel. Its backdrop is a rapidly changing world, and four days before the book was published this sense of change accelerated when the World Trade Center in New York was destroyed.

The plot centres on a dysfunctional Midwest family trying to bring their children together for one final Christmas. The title is a recurring motif throughout the novel, as characters try to correct their faults and lifestyles to accommodate one another. On a macro level, the corrections refer to a broad spectrum, from neurological rewiring to stock-market adjustments. It's the ripples created by these corrections and the selfish motivations behind them that the book explores. Franzen doesn't shirk from the big topics; the subtext examines the morality of greed and the effects of debilitating illness. Yet all this is not to say that the novel lacks humour – in fact, it's the use of comedy in the face of adversity that characterizes its best passages. *The Corrections* is perhaps the last of the 'great American novels' written before the world changed on 9/11.

WHAT THE CRITICS SAID

'Think of the book as a blend of postmodern meganovel and Victorian family saga.' – *Raleigh News and Observer*

DISCUSSION POINTS

- Are all the themes Franzen explores universal, or are certain corrections too American to resonate with non-US audiences? Did you feel the European chapter fitted naturally with the rest of the novel? Was it an attempt to downplay the American-centric narrative?

- How much compassion do you feel for Alfred and Enid Lambert? Is the generation gap growing ever wider? To what extent does technology create this division in the novel?

- *The New York Times* said of the book: 'If you don't end up liking each one of Franzen's people, you probably just don't like people.' Do you feel this is a true statement, or is the opposite true?

- In a novel populated by largely unlikeable characters, with whom do your sympathies ultimately lie?

BACKGROUND INFORMATION

- *The Corrections* won the 2001 National Book Award for Fiction and was included in *Time* magazine's list of All-Time 100 Novels.

- Franzen was the first novelist to express dissatisfaction with Oprah's Book Club, in a bid to promote his novel as a highbrow read. This action ignited a debate in the US regarding highbrow versus mainstream literature. Arguably, it influenced Oprah's selection process thereafter, with a greater emphasis on classic books.

- A film of the novel is currently in pre-production.

SUGGESTED COMPANION BOOKS

- *Saturday* by IAN MCEWAN – a British take on dysfunctional family relationships and dealing with a parent's debilitating illness.

- *Underworld* by DON DELILLO – a similarly panoramic novel about family and society in America.

Love in the Time of Cholera

GABRIEL GARCÍA MÁRQUEZ

Published 1985 / Length 348 pages

Musing on change and chance, this is a story about love across the ages told with terrific skill. The elegant formality of Márquez's prose conjures a bygone era of civility and propriety, courtship and concealment. From his study of a marriage to his sketch of a widow locked into routines of remembrance, Márquez makes his characters complex beings with extensive inner lives. He introduces us to his three protagonists – queenlike, statuesque Fermina Daza, upstanding professional Juvenal Urbino and lovelorn Florentino Ariza – through a series of episodes and encounters, refusing to 'sum them up', thus displaying the consummate respect a great novelist has for his creations. The rare instances of reported speech in the book erupt as a culmination of the thoughts and feelings of both speaker and listener, to which we have already been privy. This technique allows the reader to fill in reams of subtext beneath the spoken words. Evocations of spaces warmed by the Caribbean sun are thick with rich description in this serene but lustrous gem of a novel.

READER'S OPINION

'There is no better introduction to the bejewelled, subtle magic of Márquez's writing, sustained by interwoven tales at once pathetic and inspired. Edith Grossman's exquisite translation allows none of the thrill of the language to escape.' – LINDA, 33

DISCUSSION POINTS

● Does Márquez see youthful and mature love as fundamentally the same or profoundly different? Is young love idealized, or impetuous? Is romantic love a victory over age?

- Márquez has said of Fermina Daza: 'She is the novel.' But does he treat her two suitors fairly? Or is this love triangle uneven from the outset?
- Social constraints, that 'tangle of conventions and prejudices', infiltrate this story of lovers, requiring them to act with courage. Is challenge the essence of romance, and have we lost something in our more permissive age?
- Why do you think the image of love as the Holy Spirit appears time and again?
- How does the novel prove – or disprove – Márquez's statement that 'nothing in this world was more difficult than love'?

BACKGROUND INFORMATION

- Márquez, a Colombian, based the book loosely around the story of his parents' courtship.
- Márquez won the Nobel Prize in Literature in 1982.
- Controversially, the author is a lifelong supporter of Fidel Castro, who keeps a home for him in Havana, Cuba.

SUGGESTED COMPANION BOOKS

- *Living to Tell the Tale* by GABRIEL GARCÍA MÁRQUEZ – this dazzling autobiography sheds light on how the author's immensely varied personal experiences shaped his preference for multilayered narratives.
- *Middlemarch* by GEORGE ELIOT – depicts a forbidden courtship sustained over time and against the odds.
- *The Nice and the Good* by IRIS MURDOCH – explores, in a thoroughly English setting, the differences between mature and immature love.

Mary Barton

ELIZABETH GASKELL

Published 1848 / Length 379 pages

'The rich man dines, while the poor man pines . . .
Would brothers do as they?'

Elizabeth Gaskell's *Mary Barton: A Tale of Manchester Life* encapsulates the lot of the middle and working classes during the 1840s, a time of social and economic turmoil. Through realistic and well-developed characters, Gaskell depicts the contrasting lives of the factory workers and their masters, juxtaposing the wealth of the latter with the poverty of the former, and showing the gradual rise of the antagonistic trade unions.

Set against this backdrop of oppression and suffering is the story of Mary Barton, the novel's romantic protagonist. We follow her character as she is seduced by the rose-coloured life of her father's enemy, rejects the love of her childhood friend, and becomes unwittingly caught up in an investigation into a violent murder. Involving comic scenes, vivid images, strong female characters, romance and crime, Gaskell engages the reader from beginning to end, posing questions that are still significant today.

READER'S OPINION

'With so much emphasis on the oppressive life of the workers during this period, it might be assumed that this is a bit of a dull read, but I found it completely the opposite. The historical insight is interesting without being too arduous and Mary is a strong and likeable character.' – VICTORIA, 22

DISCUSSION POINTS

● The title of the novel is *Mary Barton*; the subtitle *A Tale of Manchester Life*. Which best sums up the story?

- Examine Gaskell's depiction of the trade unions. To what extent do you think she agreed with their ideas?
- Mary and Alice are two of the strongest characters in the novel. Do you think that the book is written from a feminist point of view?
- A strong theme is the question of 'nature versus nurture' – the narrator likens the 'uneducated' to the monster in *Frankenstein*, because without education they have no moral grasp of good and evil. How far would you agree that knowledge of good and evil is taught?

BACKGROUND INFORMATION

- Gaskell was the first novelist to replicate the working-class language of Manchester in literary form, and went further than any other contemporary writer in depicting the appalling plight of the industrial poor of the 1840s.
- Gaskell lived in Manchester, where she was involved in charity work and spent time trying to help the poor.
- *Mary Barton* was a successful debut. Gaskell went on to write forty-eight more works, including *North and South* (1855), which was made into a BBC TV drama in 2004.

SUGGESTED COMPANION BOOKS

- *Frankenstein* by MARY SHELLEY – deals with the question of nature versus nurture.
- *North and South* by ELIZABETH GASKELL – follows the journey of another romantic heroine during the upheavals in the 1840s industrial North.
- *The Ragged Trousered Philanthropists* by ROBERT TRESSELL – a socialist classic examining the impact of capitalism and trade unions on the working class.

Cold Comfort Farm

STELLA GIBBONS
Published 1932 / Length 307 pages

Cold Comfort Farm is a delicious satire on the tradition of doom-laden rural melodramas that runs from the works of the Brontës and Thomas Hardy to those of Mary Webb and D. H. Lawrence. Flora Poste, a thoroughly modern young woman accustomed to the sophisticated social whirl of London, descends upon her relatives – the extraordinarily gloomy Starkadders – and takes them in hand with reforming zeal. Flora approaches each member of the sprawling Starkadder clan as a human puzzle, to be solved in a satisfactory manner with her trademark composure and supreme good sense. Her schemes include everyone, from brooding local Lothario, Seth, right up to the benighted lunatic matriarch Aunt Ada Doom (who once saw 'something nasty in the woodshed', and has never recovered). Much more than a simple lampoon of its literary antecedents, *Cold Comfort Farm* is a gorgeously enjoyable novel. Stella Gibbons's narration is deft and extremely funny, and she elevates many, if not all, of her characters above the level of simple archetypes. The language sparkles with ingenuity and there are phrases of superb comedy that beg to be read out loud.

READER'S OPINION

'A friend once told me that I reminded him of Flora Poste. I was delighted – though I'm not sure I should have been. I love her style, though I have to confess to some reservations about the way in which she takes it upon herself to reconfigure her relatives' personalities and fates.' – ANA, 29

DISCUSSION POINTS

- Why do you think Gibbons chose to set the book 'in the near future'? How has the book dated since its publication in 1932?

- Is Flora a sympathetic character? What motivates her, and what disturbs her composure? Does she ultimately learn anything from her cousins?
- Do you feel that urban society is held up as an ideal in the book?
- There's no answer to this, but it's great fun anyway: what was in the woodshed?

BACKGROUND INFORMATION

- Gibbons was inspired to write the book after working on an extract from Webb's *The Golden Arrow* for the *Evening Standard* in 1928. She said in *Punch* in 1966, 'The large agonized faces in Mary Webb's book annoyed me . . . I did not believe people were any more despairing in Herefordshire than in Camden Town.'
- *Cold Comfort Farm* was adapted for television in 1968, starring Sarah Bedel, and in 1995, starring Kate Beckinsale; it was also adapted for the stage in 1991. In addition, it inspired the record 'Something for the Weekend' by The Divine Comedy.
- Although Gibbons wrote several other novels, she is remembered largely for this book alone.

SUGGESTED COMPANION BOOKS

- *Wuthering Heights* by EMILY BRONTË – tragic lovers wailing across a harsh rural landscape that echoes their emotional turmoil.
- *Women in Love* by D. H. LAWRENCE – Gibbons parodies Lawrence's style in *Cold Comfort Farm*, especially in her portrayal of Seth and his animal magnetism.
- *Breakfast at Tiffany's* by TRUMAN CAPOTE – an inversion: a country girl plays the gilded urban sophisticate.

Lord of the Flies

William Golding

Published 1954 / Length 223 pages

A modern classic, Golding's compelling debut novel is an allegorical fable about original sin: 'the darkness of man's heart'. In the midst of an unspecified war, a group of pre-pubescent schoolboys are stranded on a tropical island when their evacuation plane crashes, with no adults around and only each other to rely on. At first, they embrace democracy and civilization as they adapt to their new surroundings. But human nature soon intervenes – with horrifying results. Populated by characters that some critics have suggested represent different aspects of the human psyche, *Lord of the Flies* is brilliantly told with incisive brevity, overtly symbolic language and unrelenting pace. The tale may focus on the microcosm of a group of boys, but its impact is far-reaching, examining the struggle between reason and animal savagery that is the universal human dilemma.

What the critics said

'This brilliant work is a frightening parody on man's return (in a few weeks) to that state of darkness from which it took him thousands of years to emerge. Fully to succeed, a fantasy must approach very close to reality. *Lord of the Flies* does. It must also be superbly written. It is.' – *The New York Times*

Discussion points

- Why do you think Golding chose to set the story on an island, and use children as his protagonists? Do these choices allow Golding to demonstrate his theory of evil? Is his theory correct?
- Discuss the symbolic meanings and journeys of such items as the conch, Piggy's glasses, the signal fire and Jack's painted face.

- Some critics argue that Simon represents Christ. What in the novel suggests this? Do you agree with this interpretation?
- How fully rounded are the characters? Do you think Golding manipulates the reader with some of his portrayals?
- What is the beast? Can it be defeated?

BACKGROUND INFORMATION

- Thirty-one publishers rejected the book before it was accepted for publication.
- Golding won the Nobel Prize in Literature in 1983. He once described the novel's theme as 'an attempt to trace the defects of society back to the defects of human nature'.
- The political situation at the time of writing was fraught – the Cold War between East and West had begun and there was a real chance of nuclear war. The novel is rooted in these concerns, with clear parallels contrasting democracy and totalitarianism.

SUGGESTED COMPANION BOOKS

- *Heart of Darkness* by JOSEPH CONRAD (see page 52) – also explores the darkness within mankind, and pits civilization against barbarity.
- *The Beach* by ALEX GARLAND – an isolated, seemingly idyllic tropical community turns on itself.
- *The Coral Island* by R. M. BALLANTYNE – *Lord of the Flies* was something of a response to this Victorian adventure story, which has a very different treatment of a similar premise.

The Tin Drum

Günter Grass

Published 1959 / Length 580 pages

A complex and intricate tour de force, and one of the outstanding achievements of twentieth-century European literature, *The Tin Drum* tells the darkly comic story of Oskar Matzerath. Based in Danzig, Poland, and later in Düsseldorf, it is told from Oskar's grotesquely warped perspective, covering the period before, during and immediately after the Second World War. Oskar is a dwarf, a fact that he attributes to his decision not to grow any larger from the age of three onwards, and throughout his life he taps out rhythms on drums, a strikingly martial soundtrack to the events that unfold. He also discovers the ability to shatter glass with his screams, a talent that he employs whenever his drumming is under threat. As he grows older, he comes to identify strongly with both Satan and Jesus. Packed with vividly drawn characters – including Oskar's two 'presumptive fathers', Alfred Matzerath and Jan Bronski, and the dwarf ringmaster Bebra – the story encompasses many themes and styles, but it always circles around the atrocities committed under the Nazis' regime and the aftermath of their time in power.

Reader's opinion

'At times it was a struggle to get through this, although the translation could have been to blame for that. It was worth persevering with, though. The disturbing imagery will stay with me for ever – particularly the horse's head used as bait to catch eels, and Oskar sitting on the Virgin Mary's knee in place of the baby Jesus.' – MATT, 26

Discussion points

- Why do you think Grass chose to tell this story of wartime

Poland from Oskar's perspective? What effect does this choice of lead character have on the nature of the story?

- Do you trust Oskar's version of events? What undermines the telling of his story?
- 'Jesus was the spit and image of Oskar.' Why does Oskar associate himself so closely with the baby Jesus?
- What does Oskar use his drum for? Why do you think Grass chose the tin drum as the novel's central symbol?

BACKGROUND INFORMATION

- Günter Grass was born and raised in Danzig, where *The Tin Drum* and two of his other novels, *The Rat* and *The Flounder*, are set.
- In 2006, he revealed that he had been a member of the Waffen-SS (condemned as a criminal organization at the Nuremberg Trials) during the Second World War. This revelation has led to accusations of hypocrisy for his anti-war stance.
- Grass received the Nobel Prize in Literature in 1999.

SUGGESTED COMPANION BOOKS

- *The Life and Opinions of Tristram Shandy, Gentleman* by LAURENCE STERNE – another quirky fictional memoir, with a similar structure and an unreliable narrator.
- *Gulliver's Travels* by JONATHAN SWIFT – satirical fiction presenting political opinion.
- *Slaughterhouse-Five* by KURT VONNEGUT – criticism of war through satire.
- *The Book Thief* by MARKUS ZUSAK (see page 222) – another unusual narrative voice giving a different perspective on the Nazi regime.

The End of the Affair

GRAHAM GREENE

Published 1951 / Length 192 pages

In post-Second World War England, novelist Maurice Bendrix is determined to discover why his ex-lover, Sarah Miles, broke off their relationship suddenly and without explanation two years previously. When the pair are briefly reunited, Maurice's old feelings resurface and he hires a private detective to follow Sarah in order to find out why and, more specifically, for whom she left him. However, his reignited passion soon turns into a destructive fixation. *The End of the Affair* is a masterful novel exploring the fine lines between love and hate, possession and loss, religious faith and human despair. It is the first of Greene's novels to present an interventionist God directly touching people's lives and performing miracles. The novel scrutinizes physical and spiritual love and the intersection between the two – a subject that is explored through the Catholic belief in the incarnated Christ. While examining the raptures of physical love, *The End of the Affair* looks beyond the transience of sexual desire to consider the eternal nature of the soul and the antagonism between flesh and spirit.

READER'S OPINION

'I like Greene's clipped style; he doesn't need flashy literary devices to convey his meaning. Beautifully written and a probing examination of human relationships, this is definitely one of my favourite books.' – KIERAN, 23

DISCUSSION POINTS

- One of the most important devices Greene employs – crucial to the plot, tone and perspective of the novel – is the switch in narrator and narrative form halfway through the novel.

What do you think is the purpose and effect of this transition?

- What motifs and devices does Greene utilize in order to explore the relationship between the physical and the spiritual? Do you think bodily and spiritual love are ultimately presented as reconcilable or conflicting forces?

- The novel's epigraph is a quotation from the French Catholic novelist Léon Bloy: 'Man has places in his heart which do not yet exist, and into them enters suffering in order that they may have existence.' What do you think is the role of suffering and its effect on personal development in the novel?

BACKGROUND INFORMATION

- The novel was based on Greene's own affair with Lady Catherine Walston, for whom he left his wife in 1948.

- Critics consider *The End of the Affair* to be the last of Greene's Catholic tetralogy, consisting of *Brighton Rock* (1938), *The Power and the Glory* (1940) and *The Heart of the Matter* (1948).

SUGGESTED COMPANION BOOKS

- *The Heart of the Matter* by GRAHAM GREENE – a long-serving police officer in a British colonial town on the west coast of Africa wrestles with the sin of pride during the First World War.

- *Brideshead Revisited* by EVELYN WAUGH (see page 216) – a similar analysis of the ways in which adultery and faith can struggle to coexist.

- *Madame Bovary* by GUSTAVE FLAUBERT – an examination of adultery and its psychological effects in nineteenth-century France.

The Secret River

KATE GRENVILLE

Published 2005 / Length 349 pages

Grenville researched her own nineteenth-century family history for the subject matter of this novel – as can be seen by reading her memoir, *Searching for the Secret River* – and it is this detailed substructure that makes this story seem so real. Anyone can make a mistake, even a bad mistake, which is exactly what the protagonist, William Thornhill, does here. In a tale that shows us the consequences of our actions, but also the opportunities that can arise from them, Thornhill is transported to New South Wales in 1806 as punishment, and is thrown into a harsh and unforgiving world he does not know. But freedom can be bought by taking up so-called 'unclaimed' land, which, in reality, is occupied by Aboriginal people. What follows is a clash of cultures, as settlers and natives try to interact. The descriptions in this book ground the reader in each of the places that Grenville visits and, in particular, provide a vivid picture of Australia. Balancing effectively competing sympathies for all parties involved, *The Secret River* is an accomplished novel that, while uncompromising, avoids over-condemnation of individuals and their actions, and allows for honest soul-searching.

WHAT THE CRITICS SAID

'*The Secret River* is a sad book, beautifully written and, at times, almost unbearable with the weight of loss, competing distresses and the impossibility of making amends.' – *The Observer*

DISCUSSION POINTS

- How realistic is the book in portraying the conflict and culture clash between settlers and natives?
- The transportation of the family to Australia is not related

in any detail. Could the book have benefited from a proper description here?

- How does this book make you view Australia, in terms of its colonization and treatment of its native people?
- How does the novel deal with the theme of guilt?
- Does the book successfully separate historical fact from myth regarding the fate of the Aboriginal people?

BACKGROUND INFORMATION

- *The Secret River* is Grenville's sixth novel. It won several awards upon its publication, including the Commonwealth Writers' Prize for Best Book, and was shortlisted for the 2006 Booker Prize.

SUGGESTED COMPANION BOOKS

- *Searching for the Secret River* by KATE GRENVILLE – a memoir telling the story of the author's research for the novel, starting with the transcript of Grenville's ancestor's 1805 Old Bailey trial, and detailing the process of turning dry research into living fiction.
- *The Inheritance of Loss* by KIRAN DESAI (see page 56) – old and new worlds clash among hope and betrayal in a crumbling house in the Himalayan foothills.
- *Remember Me* by LESLEY PEARSE – tells the story of Mary Broad, who in 1786 was one of the first people to be transported to Australia.
- *A Short History of Tractors in Ukrainian* by MARINA LEWYCKA – two feuding sisters unite to save their ageing father from a gold-digging woman, uncovering fifty years of dark European history along the way.

Top Ten Men's Books

A study in 2006 by British cultural historians Jardine and Watkins found that 80 per cent of men interviewed had most recently read a novel by a male author, and many male respondents had difficulty recalling the last book by a woman they'd read. Anecdotal evidence also suggests that some male book group members turn their noses up at books written by, or perceived to be aimed at, women. Here, then, is a list to satisfy those hunter-gatherers after more manly tomes.

Money by MARTIN AMIS

The Three Musketeers by ALEXANDRE DUMAS

American Psycho by BRET EASTON ELLIS

From Russia with Love by IAN FLEMING

High Fidelity by NICK HORNBY

Haunted by CHUCK PALAHNIUK
(contains the short story 'Guts', at the author readings
of which more than sixty people are rumoured
to have fainted)

Man and Boy by TONY PARSONS

Ivanhoe by SIR WALTER SCOTT

Filth by IRVINE WELSH

The Bonfire of the Vanities by TOM WOLFE

Top Ten Non-Fiction Books

There's nothing like curling up on the sofa with a good book. But that book doesn't have to be fiction – some of the best stories ever told are authentic fact. Here are some of the most memorable, gripping, chilling and inspiring non-fiction books around.

Tuesdays with Morrie by MITCH ALBOM

In Cold Blood by TRUMAN CAPOTE

Wild Swans: Three Daughters of China
by JUNG CHANG

A Heartbreaking Work of Staggering Genius
by DAVE EGGERS

The Diary of Anne Frank by ANNE FRANK

*Don't Let's Go to the Dogs Tonight:
An African Childhood*
by ALEXANDRA FULLER

Goodbye to All That by ROBERT GRAVES

If This Is a Man by PRIMO LEVI

And When Did You Last See Your Father?
by BLAKE MORRISON

Longitude by DAVA SOBEL

Twenty Thousand Streets Under the Sky

PATRICK HAMILTON

Published 1935 / Length 528 pages

This trilogy comprises three self-contained volumes that link thematically and through overlapping characters; each was published separately before being collected. All three tales centre on a pub and tell the same story from different perspectives, exposing the lives of people on the margins of 1930s London society. *The Midnight Bell*, an examination of obsession, is the most autobiographical and provides moving insight into the emotional damage of the author's life. *The Siege of Pleasure* follows the descent of a servant girl into prostitution, a woman whose beauty captivates Bob, who yearns for both emotional and financial security like so many of Hamilton's characters. *The Plains of Cement* traces the dreams harboured by barmaid Ella of escaping her social class and reaching a world elsewhere. Hamilton is marvellous at evoking his era in all its variety, both the upper and lower classes of his city, those at the bright heart of society and those flitting around its fringes.

READER'S OPINION

'I hugely enjoyed reading this, although I'm not sure "enjoy" is the right word, as the author conjures such a bleak world. The author gained my sympathy for the characters, the language was a delight and I often think of scenes when I am in pubs.' – LISA, 29

DISCUSSION POINTS

- 'I can't stand cruelty,' says Jenny Maple. What forms of cruelty are portrayed? Is Hamilton a ruthless writer, or does he depict kindness too? Which are the unavoidable cruelties and which purposefully inflicted?

- 'For a moment he had been a racked soul contemplating itself in a pitch-dark and irrevocable Universe' – to what extent does Hamilton suggest the human capability to change situations, and to what extent are they presented as 'irrevocable'?
- How does Hamilton explore youth and age, and the conflicts between the life of the body and the life of the mind?
- Bob describes a 'vile and disappointing planet'. To what extent is that the overall mood of the writing?

BACKGROUND INFORMATION

- Patrick Hamilton wrote this London trilogy when in his mid and late twenties.
- In January 1932, Hamilton was knocked down by a car and critically injured. He added this experience to the final draft of *The Siege of Pleasure*, so that emotional and psychological wounds were also comparable to physical ones.
- *The Midnight Bell* is based on Hamilton's own disastrous love affair with a prostitute.

SUGGESTED COMPANION BOOKS

- The *Gorse* novels by PATRICK HAMILTON – in the early 1950s, Hamilton wrote a series of disturbing novels focusing on a sociopathic protagonist.
- *Patrick Hamilton: A Life* by SEAN FRENCH and *Through a Glass Darkly: The Life of Patrick Hamilton* by NIGEL JONES – Hamilton's experiences had such influence on his writing that it is interesting to read his life and work together. These 1990s biographies offer insight.
- *Vile Bodies* by EVELYN WAUGH – a satirical novel capturing the decadence of 1930s London.

Five Quarters of the Orange

Joanne Harris
Published 2001 / Length 363 pages

Five Quarters of the Orange is a dark, bitter tale of shattered lives and lost loves in rural France during the Second World War. We see the scenes of betrayal and retribution unfolding through the eyes of a nine-year-old girl, Framboise, who, as mistress of her rural world, fishes obsessively in the river while she struggles to cope with her increasingly tyrannical and migraine-ridden mother and builds a rapport with a soldier from the occupying German Army, Thomas Leibniz. The tastes, textures and meaning of food inhabit the book; the scent of oranges especially pervades it, as Framboise exploits its capacity to incapacitate her mother (for reasons we begin to guess at), thus providing Framboise and her siblings with opportunities to escape their mother's controlling clutches. But when the children do elude her influence, they are in wartime France. In such an environment, small misadventures become writ large. As the plot twists and turns to the fireworks of the climax, so it proves. *Five Quarters of the Orange* is an engrossing story of mothers and daughters, of old loves made anew, of revenge and hatred.

READER'S OPINION

'It's a real page-turner – every bit as captivating as *Chocolat*, but much darker and all the more rewarding for that. The interlacing of recipes with plot is intriguing, but the invented language is rather annoying, so it's just as well it makes only brief appearances.' – JAMES, 53

DISCUSSION POINTS

● Are these children especially wicked, or are their wicked actions merely amplified because it is wartime?

- What are we expected to believe Thomas Liebniz's motivation is for spending so much time with the children, and especially with Framboise?

- What conclusions do you draw from the book about the nature of childhood then and now? Consider the issues of freedom and control.

- As in Harris's other books, food is portrayed as an agent in society, a force in its own right – although in this case a negative rather than a positive one, as in *Chocolat*. How well do the descriptions of food fit the narrative?

BACKGROUND INFORMATION

- *Five Quarters of the Orange* was Harris's follow-up book to the hugely successful *Chocolat* (1999), which made her a household name.

- The novel is based on the experiences of Harris's French maternal grandfather, who had been decorated in the war, but was then denounced to the Gestapo by an acquaintance who was in the Resistance. As a result, the family were forced to flee and hide away on a relative's distant farm.

SUGGESTED COMPANION BOOKS

- *Chocolat* by JOANNE HARRIS – this is a perfect sweet complement to the bitterness of *Five Quarters*.

- *Like Water for Chocolate* by LAURA ESQUIVEL – food and cooking dominate another tale of mothers and daughters.

- *Captain Corelli's Mandolin* by LOUIS DE BERNIÈRES (see page 54) – similar scenes of a small rural world caught up in the larger geo-political battle of the Second World War.

The Go-Between

L. P. HARTLEY
Published 1953 / Length 280 pages

The Go-Between is a story of ill-fated love, snobbery and black magic, viewed through the eyes of an old man, Leo Colston, looking back on his youth. Leo is spending the long, hot summer of 1900 at the Norfolk home of his aristocratic friend Marcus. Marcus's sister Marian recruits Leo to carry messages between her and a local farmer, Ted Burgess. Leo gradually becomes obsessed with the beautiful Marian, but she is engaged to Lord Trimingham, and he comes to realize that her relationship with Ted is doomed. As the heat of the summer builds, Leo is caught up in the emotional manipulation of the two lovers and the demands of social propriety, and begins to interfere in their communications – with tragic consequences. Matters draw to a head on the eve of Leo's thirteenth birthday, when he sets in train a sequence of events that will blight his life for ever.

WHAT THE CRITICS SAID

'Like Henry James, his most obvious literary forebear, Hartley examines the nuances of morality with a shimmering exactness, focusing on characters . . . caught between natural impulses and the social conventions that would thwart them.' – *The New York Times*

DISCUSSION POINTS

- The famous opening line of the book is: 'The past is a foreign country; they do things differently there.' Is the author trying to warn us not to judge the characters by the standards of our own time? Or is he trying to explain the emotional distance between the adult narrator and the Leo of the action?

- What are we to make of Leo's magic spells, of the naming of characters after zodiac signs and the frequent discussion of the zodiac? What does this bring to the book?

- How well or badly is Leo treated by the Maudsleys and by Ted? Does any character in the book really like him as a person, or are they all using him for their own ends?

- How might Leo have matured if the affair had turned out differently? Would his life still have been shaped by the events of that summer?

- Are any of the characters responsible for their own actions, or are they all forced to behave in the way they do because of the demands of their social standing?

BACKGROUND INFORMATION

- Harold Pinter adapted *The Go-Between* in 1971 for the film of the same name starring Julie Christie and Alan Bates.

SUGGESTED COMPANION BOOKS

- *The Great Gatsby* by F. SCOTT FITZGERALD (see page 72) – explores similar themes of doomed love and social class, set twenty years later in America.

- *The Gambler* by FYODOR DOSTOEVSKY – another story dealing with characters who are driven to extremes of behaviour by forces seemingly beyond their control.

- *To Kill a Mockingbird* by HARPER LEE (see page 130) – a juvenile narrator comes to terms with the darker side of the adult world.

The Scarlet Letter

Nathaniel Hawthorne
Published 1850 / Length 228 pages

Boston, seventeenth century. A beautiful young woman, Hester Prynne, is released from prison and forced to stand on a scaffold under the stern Puritan gaze of her fellow townspeople. In her arms is her illegitimate baby, and on her breast is pinned a scarlet piece of cloth in the shape of the letter A (for adulteress), which she is condemned to wear for the rest of her life. She refuses to name the child's father, and is cast out by her society. Meanwhile, a stranger in the crowd appears to recognize her . . .

This dramatic scene opens *The Scarlet Letter*, and sets the stage for what is to follow. The story of Hester, and her dignified struggle against the social mores of the day, has become one of the great classics of American literature. Part psychological drama, part melodrama, it explores the gulf between public shame and private guilt, and how one can never escape the consequences of one's actions.

READER'S OPINION

'It's an odd novel, in which the key event – Hester's love affair – has occurred before the story begins. It's set in a society whose values are utterly alien to ours and, indeed, were alien in the author's time. And it's wildly melodramatic in places. But for all that, it's an absorbing read, though I found the Preface rather dull.' – SUZIE, 35

DISCUSSION POINTS

- Are the moral dilemmas faced by the characters in this book at all relevant to a modern society?
- Hawthorne made the distinction between the atmospheric 'romance', which this is, and the realistic 'novel'. Yet the

Preface proposes it is a true story. Do you think he intends the book to be realistic?

- What do you think is the author's attitude to the Puritans, and to the father of Hester's child?
- Is this a feminist book?

BACKGROUND INFORMATION

- The book starts with a Preface, 'The Custom-House', which purports to describe how the author found the actual scarlet letter and papers documenting Hester's story, while working at the custom house in Salem, Massachusetts. Hawthorne did work there, between 1846 and 1849, but there is no evidence that this story is true.
- *The Scarlet Letter* was one of the first mass-produced books in America. It was immediately hailed as a classic, though it sold fewer than 8,000 copies in the author's lifetime.
- There have been numerous film adaptations of the story, most recently a 1995 version starring Demi Moore and Gary Oldman.

SUGGESTED COMPANION BOOKS

- *The Crucible*, a play by ARTHUR MILLER – a shocking tragedy set in intolerant Puritan society (incidentally, Hawthorne's ancestors were directly involved in the Salem witchcraft trials).
- *Tess of the D'Urbervilles* by THOMAS HARDY – another woman living with the consequences of her supposed sin, written some forty years after *The Scarlet Letter*.
- *Crime and Punishment* by FYODOR DOSTOEVSKY – a masterly exploration of the destructive internal effects of guilt.

Catch-22

JOSEPH HELLER
Published 1961 / Length 544 pages

Catch-22 is a satirical novel set during the Second World War, which tells the story of Captain Yossarian, a member of the US Army Air Force, and his attempts to guarantee his own personal safety by evading a war in which he has been forced to participate. In Heller's book, Catch-22 is an unwritten military law, which allows senior officers to prevent airmen from being excused from flying missions. Airmen could be grounded by being declared insane, but with one catch: Catch-22. As the squadron's physician Doc Daneeka explains, 'Orr would be crazy to fly more missions and sane if he didn't, but if he was sane he had to fly them. If he flew them he was crazy and didn't have to; but if he didn't want to he was sane and had to.'

Although the main targets of Heller's venom are the absurdity of war, patriotism and the military establishment, he clearly has other grudges to bear. Through the character of the company's entrepreneurial mess officer, Milo Minderbinder, Heller takes sarcastic pokes at war profiteering, bureaucracy, capitalism and America's use of agricultural subsidies. Despite the fact that the elliptical, and in parts repetitive, writing style is not universally popular with readers, *Catch-22* is regarded by many as one of the great novels of the twentieth century.

READER'S OPINION

'*Catch-22* is an extremely funny and wholly original novel. Dark, surreal and in parts verging on the grotesque, *Catch-22* appealed greatly to my subversive side.' – ANDY, 29

DISCUSSION POINTS

● Are Heller's opinions on war and the military overly critical?

- Does the satirical style adequately present Heller's anti-war arguments?
- The book is often referred to as an archetypal 'boys' book'. Does it hold any appeal for female readers?
- Does *Catch-22* offer any solutions, or merely highlight problems?
- How does *Catch-22* compare to later war novels? Is it still relevant today?

BACKGROUND INFORMATION

- The phrase 'catch-22' comes from Joseph Heller's novel. The book was originally entitled *Catch-18*, but this had to be changed so it would not be confused with another recently published Second World War novel (*Mila 18* by Leon Uris).
- Initial critical opinion of the book was quite divided. *The New Yorker* said that it 'doesn't even seem to be written; instead, it gives the impression of having been shouted on to paper . . . what remains is a debris of sour jokes'.

SUGGESTED COMPANION BOOKS

- *Slaughterhouse-Five* by KURT VONNEGUT – with a darkly comic literary style similar to Heller's, the main themes of Vonnegut's classic are also war and the loss of individual free will.
- *The Thin Red Line* by JAMES JONES – another Second World War novel, in which the characters shown in the most positive light are those most cynical towards the war.
- *Nineteen Eighty-Four* by GEORGE ORWELL (see page 158) – explores the forfeiture of individual freedom to the collective good.
- *Closing Time* by JOSEPH HELLER – the sequel to *Catch-22*, which follows the future lives of some of the characters.

Notes on a Scandal

ZOË HELLER

Published 2003 / Length 256 pages

Lonely history teacher Barbara Covett has few friends and no confidantes when beautiful Bathsheba Hart breezes into her life. Seizing the opportunity for companionship, Barbara sets about making herself indispensable to the naive Sheba in order to fill 'the white wastelands' of her 'appointmentless weeks'. Heller's second novel is filtered through the eyes of spinster Barbara, who takes an almost voyeuristic delight in recording the minutiae of her daily encounters in her journals. It quickly emerges that she is neither a reliable nor dispassionate narrator, and when pottery teacher Sheba engages in an illicit affair, it is gradually revealed just how well practised Barbara is in the art of manipulation. With delightful cameos from maths teacher Brian Bangs and enthusiastic headmaster Sandy Pabblem, this is a witty, dark and poignant account of two women searching for fulfilment. Most interesting is the way in which the pivotal 'scandal' is not sensationalized, nor are we required to pass judgement; instead, one taboo gives way to another, leading to a fascinating foray into the power of obsession.

WHAT THE CRITICS SAID

'Heller is a fine writer, fashioning her material with supreme confidence: the novel is funny, bleak, superbly structured, and full of the satisfyingly tight phrases that distinguish her journalism, but the fundamental point is somehow elusive.' – *The Guardian*

DISCUSSION POINTS

- Max Davidson commented in his review: 'Not many newspaper columnists adapt to the more strenuous demands of writing novels. Heller is the exception who proves the rule.' Do you think her transition from journalist to novelist is successful? Is it easy to detect that she is a journalist in the way she writes?

- Consider the book's title. In what way is its simplicity either apt or ill-fitting given the narrator's character? Is the 'scandal' to which it refers simply Sheba's affair?

- Has Heller produced characters worthy of our sympathy as well as our contempt? Is there any vulnerability in Barbara that endears her to the reader?

BACKGROUND INFORMATION

- The novel was shortlisted for the 2003 Booker Prize.

- It was released as a feature film in 2006, directed by Richard Eyre and starring Cate Blanchett and Judi Dench.

- The book was selected for the first *Richard & Judy* Book Club reading list in 2004.

SUGGESTED COMPANION BOOKS

- *Drowning Ruth* by CHRISTINA SCHWARZ (see page 182) – a comparable controlling central character.

- *The Aspern Papers* by HENRY JAMES – the narrator's need for fulfilment leads to an uncontrollable obsession.

- *Love Lessons* by JACQUELINE WILSON – a fifteen-year-old's perspective on a pupil–teacher relationship.

To Have and Have Not

Ernest Hemingway

Published 1937 / Length 180 pages

To Have and Have Not is a work of thrilling subtropical action. The central character, Harry Morgan, is one of Hemingway's famous macho men. He's a hard drinker and tough talker who is forced, by poverty and circumstance, into rum-running and people-smuggling from the dangerous coast of Cuba to the Florida Keys. Around him circle a collection of characters for whom penury, alcoholism, failed love affairs and casual violence are a way of life. Although *To Have and Have Not* is often regarded as one of Hemingway's weakest novels, this critical viewpoint does not take into account the darkness and depth of the book. So much more than just a thriller set in the thirties, it examines a community for whom the American dream has failed. The writing is frequently understated, yet characters are unafraid to register emotion in the face of crisis. Ultimately, the novel is about the human urge to survive, and the problem of fighting only for yourself in an interdependent society.

WHAT THE CRITICS SAID

'[*To Have and Have Not*] . . . shows extraordinary mastery of the art of indirect exposition of character . . . In life, our ideas of other persons are inferences based on what they say and do. Hemingway chooses to let us learn about his characters in the same way.' – GRANVILLE HICKS, *The New Yorker*

DISCUSSION POINTS

● Is Harry Morgan a sympathetic character? How does his marked racism affect modern audiences?

● The story is told from several different points of view: why do you think this is? How successful is it?

- Why do you think Hemingway included the professors and their marital disputes? Do they help to make a point about the 'haves' and the 'have nots'?

- As the famous quotation from John Donne's 'Meditation XVII' states: 'No man is an island.' Do Harry's words at the end of the book offer the reader any kind of resolution? What do they even mean?

- Critics have often accused *To Have and Have Not* of being several short stories strung together, rather than an entire novel. Is there a coherence to or general message throughout the whole work?

Background information

- Ernest Hemingway is one of the most famous twentieth-century American authors, credited with helping shape what is considered to be the 'American style': understated description from ambiguous narrators.

- *To Have and Have Not* was written at the end of a dark period for the USA: in 1934, the Depression had depleted the national average income by 40 per cent and Prohibition had proved an unsuccessful experiment in taking away the one thing – alcohol – that had kept many happy.

Suggested companion books

- *Diamonds are Forever* by IAN FLEMING – another thriller with a similarly complex central character.

- *Jamaica Inn* by DAPHNE DU MAURIER – alcoholism and smuggling in nineteenth-century Cornwall.

- *Our Man in Havana* by GRAHAM GREENE – set during the corrupt pre-Castro Cuban regime, twenty years after the events of *To Have and Have Not*.

This Book Will Save Your Life

A. M. Homes
Published 2006 / Length 372 pages

Set in modern-day Los Angeles, *This Book Will Save Your Life* charts a summer in the life of Richard Novak, a successful but emotionally numb share trader who rarely leaves the air-conditioned luxury of his house high up in the Hollywood hills. The day before the novel opens he suffers an inexplicable and intense pain resulting in hospitalization; when he returns to his house, he notices a huge hole has opened up in the ground nearby. The foundations of his ordered world are literally and metaphorically shifting.

During the course of the book, we follow Richard's journey through a seemingly random progression of events and inter-actions with a cast of unusual and often eccentric characters. The setting adds to the heightened, almost surreal atmosphere – this is a strange, wild LA filled with feral chihuahuas, landslides, bush fires, a stranded horse and a mystery big cat. Homes's eco-nomical writing style is filled with sharp, black humour: it may be an 'easy' read, but it packs a strong emotional punch.

What the critics said

'The book is a gentle, entertaining antidote to the overachieve-ments of much of modern life . . . Overall, it is fantastical, anti-American, anti-consumerist, anti-individualist.' – *The Observer*

Discussion points

- It's unusual in literature for the soul-searching hero to be so wealthy. What importance does money have on Richard's emotional journey? Did you find that his wealth hindered you from identifying with him?

- The author has talked about her strong sense of 'dislocation' in being an adopted child (as described in her memoir, *The Mistress's Daughter*). How is Richard 'dislocated' from his own life at the start of the novel? Do you think it's useful to look at an author's real life when you're thinking about their work?

- Most of the major characters in the book are men. Do you think the (female) author captures the male psyche successfully?

- Did this book save your life? What is the relevance of the title?

BACKGROUND INFORMATION

- *This Book Will Save Your Life* was selected as a *Richard & Judy* Book Club choice in 2007.

SUGGESTED COMPANION BOOKS

- *The Great Gatsby* by F. SCOTT FITZGERALD (see page 72) – a powerful portrayal of the souring of the American dream, set in the jazz age.

- *The Bonfire of the Vanities* by TOM WOLFE – a successful Wall Street trader's life unravels as the result of a random event.

- *Less Than Zero* by BRET EASTON ELLIS – career-launching novel depicting the nihilistic world of the privileged in 1980s Los Angeles.

The Kite Runner

Khaled Hosseini

Published 2003 / Length 336 pages

The Kite Runner is an epic tale of friendship and betrayal, and of the need for love and redemption. Motherless Amir and Hassan belong to the same prosperous household in Afghanistan's capital, Kabul. Yet their relationship is not one of equals: though they are raised together, they are divided by social and religious standing. Acutely aware that he falls short of paternal expectations, Amir enters the annual kite-fighting competition in a desperate bid to impress his father. With Hassan – the best kite runner in town – at his side, Amir feels invincible. Yet this is the day that Amir will witness a terrible act, and both boys' lives will change for ever. Years later, Amir receives a phone call that he cannot ignore, a call to return to Afghanistan, where a shocking truth awaits him – as does his chance to make good.

What the critics said

'Hosseini is . . . the first Afghan novelist to fictionalize his culture for a Western readership, melding the personal struggle of ordinary people into the terrible historical sweep of a devastated country in a rich and soul-searching narrative . . . about the price of peace, both personal and political, and what we knowingly destroy in our hope of achieving that, be it friends, democracy or ourselves.' – *The Observer*

Discussion points

- As an adult, Amir tells us that everything that transpired had its foundation in his and Hassan's first words: 'Mine was Baba. His was Amir.' What do you think he means by this?
- Compare the relationships between fathers and sons in the novel.

- 'When you tell a lie, you steal someone's right to the truth.' How might Amir respond to the maxim his father impressed on him as a child upon his return to Afghanistan?

- Discuss the role of Rahim Khan in the novel.

- What does the novel have to say about Afghanistan pre- and post-Taliban rule? Compare and contrast life in Afghanistan and America for Amir and Baba and the changes it effects in both men.

BACKGROUND INFORMATION

- Hosseini was born in Afghanistan and his family received political asylum in the USA in 1980. *The Kite Runner* is his first novel, and was a word-of-mouth sensation, selling over 8 million copies. It remained on *The New York Times* bestseller list for two years.

- The Penguin/Orange Reading Group competition voted *The Kite Runner* Reading Group Book of the Year in 2006.

SUGGESTED COMPANION BOOKS

- *The Bookseller of Kabul* by ASNE SEIERSTAD (see page 186) – a Western journalist moves into the home of a Kabul bookseller just after the fall of the Taliban, and experiences firsthand what family life is like in the newly liberated city.

- *What I Loved* by SIRI HUSTVEDT – two men become friends in 1970s New York and their lives become intertwined, including their relationships with their sons, who are born in the same year.

Atomised

MICHEL HOUELLEBECQ
Published 1998 / Length 384 pages

'An age that was miserable and troubled. Often haunted by misery, the men of his generation lived out their lonely, bitter lives.'

A dark mood pervades this controversial French novel, which follows the lives of two half-brothers. Michel Djerzinski is considered a first-rate biologist, a candidate for the Nobel Prize, but he's losing his grip, and takes a year off from his work. Whereas he withdraws from life, his half-brother, Bruno, is a sensualist. Although opposites, they are both refugees from a miserable reality. The novel is a damning indictment of a society in which social connections have fragmented into individualism. Houellebecq explores biology, politics and new-age philosophies in a narrative that has become notorious for its graphic depictions of sex in its starkest form. In *Atomised*, sex is rarely linked with love, but is instead presented as a basic, often embarrassing function, which carries little pleasure. Nevertheless, it obsesses Bruno. Houellebecq offers some hope in fleeting romances that promise greater fulfilment, but his outlook, always portrayed with great energy, is ultimately unremittingly bleak and angry.

WHAT THE CRITICS SAID

'Do we take Houellebecq seriously? *Atomised* is so complex in its subject matter, and yet so excessively repulsive in its execution, that it verges, at times, on adolescent foot-stamping. It allows little room for the reader to take issue with it, so defiantly pessimistic are its parameters and its conclusions.' – *The Guardian*

DISCUSSION POINTS

- The title alludes to the 'atomisation' of society. What are some of the reasons for this atomisation?

- 'His entire adolescence was a disaster', it is said of Bruno. To what extent are these characters shaped by their childhoods? Is it possible for them to escape their pasts?

- 'Feelings such as love and tenderness and human fellowship had, for the most part, disappeared; the relationships between his contemporaries were at best indifferent and more often cruel.' Is the author's vision entirely desolate? What love and tenderness can be found in the novel, even in the midst of cruelty?

- How convincing did you find the ending of the book?

BACKGROUND INFORMATION

- *Atomised* won the 1998 Prix Novembre, one of France's most prestigious literary prizes, and the 2002 International IMPAC Dublin Literary Award. The novel has been translated into twenty-five languages.

- In 1998, Houellebecq received the Grand Prix National des Lettres Jeunes Talents for his entire body of work.

- Houellebecq's childhood was similar to that portrayed in the novel (he had an elder half-sister, and his parents were uninterested in him). The protagonists are interpreted by some as reflective of the author's own self.

SUGGESTED COMPANION BOOKS

- *Brave New World* by ALDOUS HUXLEY (see page 114) – a dystopian novel set in London and influential on Houellebecq.

- *American Psycho* by BRET EASTON ELLIS – graphic sexual and violent content; another of Houellebecq's influences.

- *The Magic Mountain* by THOMAS MANN – a philosophical novel set in a sanatorium, and Houellebecq's favourite book.

- *Politics* by ADAM THIRLWELL – a contemporary British novel with sex on its mind.

Brave New World

ALDOUS HUXLEY

Published 1932 / Length 288 pages

'I wanted to change the world. But I have found that the only thing one can be sure of changing is oneself.' – ALDOUS HUXLEY

Brave New World is set in the year of Our Ford 632: 632 years after Henry Ford created the first mass-produced car, the Model T, and became the deity of humankind. The novel describes a society based on the principles of 'community, identity and stability', in which families have been eliminated and citizens are both biologically and psychologically conditioned to accept their station in life with pleasure. There is a great deal of ambivalence throughout: there are both advantages and perils to the World State's system. Bernard Marx, a high-ranking individual unhappy with his lot, travels to one of the few Savage Reservations – where the expense of bringing 'civilization' as this world knows it has been deemed too great – and observes the human chaos of 'pre-Ford' life.

WHAT THE CRITICS SAID

'In *Nineteen Eighty-Four* . . . people are controlled by inflicting pain. In *Brave New World*, they are controlled by inflicting pleasure. In short, Orwell feared that what we hate will ruin us. Huxley feared that what we love will ruin us.' – Neil Postman, *Amusing Ourselves to Death* (1986)

DISCUSSION POINTS

- It has been suggested that, as *Brave New World* is primarily a novel of ideas, the characters are unconvincing and merely symbolic. Do you agree?
- The World State aims to eliminate emotional partnerships and the notion of family – why is this?

- How many of Huxley's predictions now look prophetic? Which major aspects of progress did he fail to anticipate?

- 'Everybody's happy now': to what extent is this true of the World State?

- Would you rather live in Huxley's London or the Savage Reservation?

BACKGROUND INFORMATION

- Like many intellectuals, Huxley expressed qualified support for eugenics in the years before the Second World War, when he was writing *Brave New World*. By the post-war period, Hitler's actions had made any such sympathies unthinkable.

- In later years, Huxley said that if he had rewritten the novel, he would have provided a third option for John, beyond the World State and the Savage Reservation.

SUGGESTED COMPANION BOOKS

- *Nineteen Eighty-Four* by GEORGE ORWELL (see page 158) / *We* by Yevgeny Zamyatin / *The Handmaid's Tale* by Margaret Atwood (see page 20) / *A Clockwork Orange* by Anthony Burgess (see page 34) – compare these visions of dystopian futures.

- *Men Like Gods* by H. G. WELLS – Huxley began *Brave New World* as a parody of this futuristic utopian novel.

- *The Tempest* by WILLIAM SHAKESPEARE – John has parallels with Caliban; the novel's title comes from one of Miranda's speeches.

- *Brave New World Revisited* (1958) by ALDOUS HUXLEY – the author revisits his novel and analyses the extent to which the modern world resembles his vision.

A Prayer for Owen Meany

JOHN IRVING

Published 1989 / Length 640 pages

Our narrator is doomed to remember Owen Meany – a boy who
is the 'colour of a gravestone' – not because of his 'wrecked
voice', nor because he was the smallest person he had ever
known, nor even because he was the reason for the narrator's
mother's death, but because it was Owen who made him believe
in God, despite his initial apathy to matters spiritual. John
Wheelright tells the story of his unusual friendship with Owen
in the 1950s and 1960s and deals with issues of fate, faith and
organized religion, set in the familiar Irving territory of a New
England school. In a tone of acquired wisdom and reflection, the
narrative features the retelling of John's and Owen's childhoods,
as well as the story of their adult lives. There is a sensuousness of
language, and humour and intellect pervade the text.

WHAT THE CRITICS SAID

'[*A Prayer For Owen Meany*] contains many of the themes found
in shots for the Great American novel – it's an anti-war Vietnam
book, it's a rites of passage book, it's a loss of innocence, blessed
childhood, where did America go wrong sort of book. . . . But
only if you're predisposed to Christian faith would you believe
in Meany; under any other circumstances, he's a dangerous and
ruthless freak with a tyrant's ability to manipulate the human
flock. [The novel] ought to be a warning about America's
dependence on heroes. But if it is, Irving has a very odd way of
going about it.' – *The Guardian*

DISCUSSION POINTS

- 'Any Christian who is not a hero is a pig' – Léon Bloy. What
  concepts of heroism does the author explore?

- How do the various characters grow in self-understanding?
- 'Have no anxiety about anything . . .' – the Letter of Paul to the Philippians. This is one of the novel's epigraphs. What are some of the anxieties that power the narrative?

BACKGROUND INFORMATION

- The 1998 feature-length film *Simon Birch*, directed by Mark Steven Johnson, was loosely based on the novel. It omitted much of the latter half and altered the ending. Irving did not believe that this novel could successfully be made into a film.
- In 2002, the Royal National Theatre staged Simon Bent's adaptation, *A Prayer for Owen Meany: On Faith*.
- The novel has seeped into cultural references. Californian punk-rock band Lagwagon based the song 'Owen Meany' on the book, as did the band Jimmy Eat World with their song 'Goodbye Sky Harbor'.

SUGGESTED COMPANION BOOKS

- *The Tin Drum* by GÜNTER GRASS (see page 86) – Owen Meany's ambiguous presence is comparable to that of the protagonist of *The Tin Drum*, Oskar Matzerath.
- *Oranges Are Not the Only Fruit* by JEANETTE WINTERSON – the central character rebels against a religious upbringing.
- *The Crucible* by ARTHUR MILLER – this play explores themes of religion and faith.

The Remains of the Day

KAZUO ISHIGURO
Published 1989 / Length 256 pages

Set after the Second World War, Ishiguro's prize-winning third novel tells the story of Stevens, an English butler, as he recalls his life through diary entries. A road trip to visit old friend Mrs Kenton triggers a series of wistful reflections on the past. Ishiguro presents the perspective of a devoted servant who believes unquestioningly in the unerring judgement of his master. The butler's insistent linguistic exactitude voices the unravelling of a bitter tragedy, as the reality of human fallibility and the fragility of ideals ultimately call him to question past actions. A failure to reconcile a sense of duty and unspoken desire, coupled with the resigned notion that 'one can't be forever dwelling on what might have been', underlie one of the most touching novels of the twentieth century. *The Remains of the Day* is a unique and profound portrayal of lost ideals, lost time and lost love, as well as a social commentary of a nation on the brink of change, conveyed through the gentle yet painful power of understatement.

READER'S OPINION

'A modern classic, and rightfully so. Essentially a book about regret, *The Remains of the Day* is both beautiful and cruel in equal measure. Stevens's road trip is wonderfully revelatory about post-war Britain. A blissful read about one man's dedication and devotion to his duty standing in the way of true happiness.' – HENRY, 24

DISCUSSION POINTS

- Does the narrative ultimately reproach Stevens for the decisions he has made? What difference does it make that he narrates his own story?

- Consider the image of Stevens's father 'searching for a precious jewel'. In what way is this symbolic of the themes and content of the novel as a whole?

- Would you regard the novel's treatment of the inner workings of an English country house as homage to traditional values, or an indictment of them?

- What do you make of Stevens's relationship with his father? Is his ability to put his professionalism before his personal crises commendable or alarming?

- In Sebastian Faulks's review, he commented: 'There is a very funny side to the butler's tale. It is not so much Stevens's pomposity, though that is quite droll in a sub-Jeeves sort of way, as the preposterous idea of the character itself.' Did you find the novel funny? If so, can you pinpoint the source of this humour?

BACKGROUND INFORMATION

- The novel won the 1989 Booker Prize.

- A 1993 film adaptation by Merchant Ivory Productions, starring Anthony Hopkins and Emma Thompson, was nominated for eight Academy Awards.

SUGGESTED COMPANION BOOKS

- *An Artist of the Floating World* by KAZUO ISHIGURO – compare the way the author deals with regret and nostalgia in post-war Japan.

- *Howards End* by E. M. FORSTER – describes a changing England and loss of ideals.

- *The Accidental Tourist* by ANNE TYLER – exploring feelings of detachment.

- *The Inimitable Jeeves* by P. G. WODEHOUSE (a collection of eleven short stories) – archetypal butler literature.

Top Ten Books
with a Younger Perspective

The *Harry Potter* phenomenon has proven that so-called kids' books have much to offer adult readers. Not only are children's books frequently rich in meaning, depth and theme, they are also often written in a way that makes their delights immediately accessible. You may find it refreshing to try one for a change, or to reacquaint yourself with an old favourite from your childhood. Here are ten wonderful books originally pitched at a younger audience that are just as stimulating and enjoyable for an older crowd.

Little Women by LOUISA MAY ALCOTT

Alice's Adventures in Wonderland by LEWIS CARROLL

The Curious Incident of the Dog in the Night-Time
by MARK HADDON

Children of the Dust by LOUISE LAWRENCE

The Chronicles of Narnia by C. S. LEWIS

The *His Dark Materials* trilogy by PHILIP PULLMAN

Swallows and Amazons by ARTHUR RANSOME

How I Live Now by MEG ROSOFF

Holes by LOUIS SACHAR

I Capture the Castle by DODIE SMITH

Top Ten Humorous Reads

We've all experienced that embarrassing yet unstoppable joy when a book makes you laugh out loud on a train, in a library or some other location where a loud guffaw is out of place. What better way to share this joy than to read a humorous book with your book club? Good comic books aren't lacking in discussion points or thought-provoking themes – and you'll all get to have a good giggle, too.

The Hitchhiker's Guide to the Galaxy
by DOUGLAS ADAMS

Lucky Jim by KINGSLEY AMIS

Three Men in a Boat by JEROME K. JEROME

Lake Wobegon Days by GARRISON KEILLOR

She's Come Undone by WALLY LAMB

The Bad Mothers' Handbook by KATE LONG

Love in a Cold Climate by NANCY MITFORD

Anita and Me by MEERA SYAL

My Life and Hard Times by JAMES THURBER
(a collection of short stories)

Thank You, Jeeves by P. G. WODEHOUSE
(the first full-length Jeeves novel)

The Turn of the Screw

Henry James
Published 1898 / Length 128 pages

The Turn of the Screw is a compelling psychological tale that focuses on the horrors faced by a new governess responsible for two young orphans at a large country house. An unnamed male narrator, whose friend possesses a manuscript purportedly written by the now dead governess some twenty years previously, reads the story to an eager audience at a Christmas gathering.

We first learn how, while settling into her new surroundings, the governess witnesses the presence of a strange man in the grounds of the house, as well as that of an unknown woman, and becomes convinced that they are the ghosts of two former employees. The welfare of her two charges, ten-year-old Miles and eight-year-old Flora, is paramount to the governess, and when she starts to fear that a malevolent force may be plaguing and corrupting them, she does everything in her power to protect the children, no matter what the cost. A fascinating and haunting read, *The Turn of the Screw* is a disturbing tale of paranoia, repression and the loss of childhood innocence.

WHAT THE CRITICS SAID

'It is a most wonderful, lurid, poisonous little tale, like an Elizabethan tragedy. I am greatly impressed by it.' – OSCAR WILDE

DISCUSSION POINTS

- Is *The Turn of the Screw* a ghost story, or the tale of an inexperienced young woman's mental breakdown?
- Did the governess's apparent attraction to her employer have an effect on the way in which she dealt with the situation at the house?

- For what reason, do you think, did Henry James choose to tell the story from the governess's point of view?
- How does James touch upon the issue of immorality in *The Turn of the Screw*?

BACKGROUND INFORMATION

- *The Turn of the Screw* was initially serialized from January to April 1898 in *Collier's Weekly*.
- James was born in New York in 1843, but moved to London in 1876, where he wrote some of his best work, including *A Portrait of a Lady* and *The Bostonians*.
- A year before his death, in 1915, James became a naturalized British citizen.

SUGGESTED COMPANION BOOKS

- *The Woman in Black* by SUSAN HILL – a junior solicitor travels to a distant estate on business, unaware of the chilling secrets that lie hidden therein.
- *Jane Eyre* by CHARLOTTE BRONTË – the story of a young and inexperienced governess in the employ of a distant and difficult man.
- *Ghost Stories of Henry James* by HENRY JAMES – a selection of chilling tales from the same author.
- *The Fall of the House of Usher and Other Stories* by EDGAR ALLEN POE – short stories of the horror genre by the master of the macabre.

The Secret Life of Bees

SUE MONK KIDD

Published 2002 / Length 384 pages

It is 1964 and the American Deep South is plagued by racial violence and civil unrest, following the passing of the Civil Rights Act. In the midst of this turbulence, fourteen-year-old Lily is struggling to cope with life with her bitter, neglectful father on their South Carolina peach farm. Lily's mother died in a tragic accident when Lily was four and, despite having only a hazy memory of the event, Lily knows that she was in some way responsible. When Lily's beloved black nanny, Rosaleen, is involved in a confrontation with three white men and is assaulted and arrested, Lily helps her to escape. With nowhere else to go, the two of them follow a trail left by Lily's mother to the town of Tiburon, where they find sanctuary with three black bee-keeping sisters. With the help of the wisdom, strength and compassion of the 'calendar sisters', Lily begins to unravel the mysteries of her mother's life and death, heal her deep-seated wounds and build a new life for herself.

WHAT THE CRITICS SAID

'Populated with rich, believable characters and propelled by a swiftly paced plot, this debut novel is a cut above most coming-of-age tales. You'll be glad you went along for the ride.' – *People*

DISCUSSION POINTS

- There is more than one mother figure in the book. Who are they? How does the parallel narrative theme of bees and bee-keeping fit in with this?

- Considering the political situation at the time, do you find it believable that Lily would be allowed to live with the three sisters?

- Did your feelings about T. Ray change as the story progressed? Were there any early hints that perhaps he was not totally unfeeling, despite his harsh treatment of Lily? Were you able to feel any sympathy for him by the end?

- Lily's feelings about her mother are complex. How do they change throughout the book? In what ways does Lily's discovery that her mother was not the perfect person she'd imagined help her to come to terms with her loss?

- What problems do you think Lily might face in the future, and what aspects of her personality might help her to overcome them?

BACKGROUND INFORMATION

- *The Secret Life of Bees* is a huge international bestseller, with over 3.5 million copies sold throughout the world. It has won numerous awards and been nominated for many more, including the prestigious Orange Prize for Fiction.

- The book is Sue Monk Kidd's debut novel. Although it is not autobiographical, she grew up in south Georgia in the 1960s and experienced the political unrest of the time.

SUGGESTED COMPANION BOOKS

- *To Kill a Mockingbird* by HARPER LEE (see page 130) – another coming-of-age story set in the Deep South and dealing with racial intolerance.

- *Divine Secrets of the Ya-Ya Sisterhood* by REBECCA WELLS – explores themes of love, family ties and female friendship.

The Girls

Lori Lansens

Published 2005 / Length 343 pages

The Girls is a beautiful novel. Poignant and moving, it's an emotional read that avoids sentimentality and never feels voyeuristic. Rose and Ruby Darlen are the oldest surviving craniopagus-conjoined twins in history. On approaching their thirtieth birthday, Rose – who has always wanted to be a writer – decides to pen her autobiography, which is where the novel begins and how it proceeds. Consequently, the main narrative is from Rose's point of view, with short interludes supplied, rather begrudgingly, by Ruby, who can't fathom why anyone would be interested in their life story. The sisters may share a body, but not a mind. They live surprisingly separate lives while, by necessity, sharing all their experiences: Rose is a sports fan and likes reading books; Ruby prefers trashy television programmes and studying local history. Above all, this book tells a story of unconditional love between two sisters, a tale that Lansens handles sensitively and compassionately.

READER'S OPINION

'This story is truly heart-warming, managing effortlessly to avoid slipping into mawkishness. In equal measures it made me laugh and cry, and introduced genuine surprises along the way.'
– DEAN, 35

DISCUSSION POINTS

- Why do you think Lansens decided to tell such a story? Is she successful in highlighting the differences in the sisters' outlooks on their life together?

- Does knowing what's to become of Ruby and Rose detract from or add to the experience of reading the novel?

- Is such subject matter difficult to convey without becoming cloying and voyeuristic? How does Lansens manage to avoid this?

- The book challenges our preconceptions of what is 'normal'. Is this uncomfortable for the reader? Can it help to break down prejudice?

- Does this novel work? That is to say, does it read as an autobiography, or as a novel written *about* conjoined twins?

BACKGROUND INFORMATION

- Lansens lives in Toronto. She is a successful screenwriter. This is her second novel.

- In preparation for writing *The Girls*, Lansens carried out research through a wide selection of literature about conjoined twins.

- In 2006, the book was nominated for the *Richard & Judy* Best Read of the Year and the Orange Prize for Fiction. *Marie Claire* named it Book of the Month.

SUGGESTED COMPANION BOOKS

- *Love in the Present Tense* by CATHERINE RYAN HYDE – how can an older man teach a young boy about 'forever love'?

- *My Sister's Keeper* by JODI PICOULT – another story about unconditional love between two sisters; its narrative, however, explores what happens when one of them questions that bond.

- *The True History of the Elephant Man* by MICHAEL HOWELL and PETER FORD – the true story of Joseph Care Merrick, who suffered from Proteus syndrome, and his experiences in Victorian England.

- *Half Life* by SHELLEY JACKSON – conjoined twins Nora and Blanche Olney star in a story that is at once funny, fierce and haunting.

Lady Chatterley's Lover

D. H. Lawrence

Published (privately) 1928
Published (unexpurgated) 1960 / Length 242 pages

Connie Reid, the novel's protagonist, leaves the cultured, bohemian life of her youth to marry Sir Clifford Chatterley, an aristocrat. Clifford and Connie enjoy a few weeks of married life before he is sent into battle in the First World War and wounded. He returns home paralysed and impotent. After Clifford begins a writing career, his house becomes a draw for intellectuals, who exhibit an emotional paralysis as powerful as the mansion owner's physical one. Connie, feeling isolated and empty, begins an unsatisfactory affair that serves only to increase her despair and desire for genuine physical connection and heartfelt passion. Connie's revulsion at her husband's loss of masculinity, both physical and spiritual, eventually leads her to become attracted to the gamekeeper, Mellors. Mellors is vital, sensual and passionate, yet also aloof and conscious of class boundaries between himself and Connie. Nevertheless, they embark on an ardent, shocking love affair. The consequences are life-changing for them both.

WHAT THE CRITICS SAID

'Ask yourselves the question: would you approve of your young sons, young daughters – because girls can read as well as boys – reading this book? Is it a book that you would have lying around the house? Is it a book you would wish your wife or servants to read?' – MERVYN GRIFFITH-JONES, for the prosecution in the *Chatterley* obscenity trial, 1960

DISCUSSION POINTS

● Is the book simply about sex between a man and a woman? Or does its message of connecting with our sexuality have something more profound to say about the nature of the human condition?

- Does Lawrence create believable characters, or does he put words into their mouths simply to articulate his own ideas – preaching rather than storytelling?
- Is the novel truly a modern one? Despite being a modernist novel in some of its themes, one could argue that the book is traditional in its structure and in some of the characters' dreams of married life.
- How successful is the book as an exploration of the English class system and the damaging effects of industrialization and materialism?

BACKGROUND INFORMATION

- *Lady Chatterley's Lover* was Lawrence's final novel.
- The book's frank sexual language and depictions of sex led to the infamous 1960 prosecution of Penguin Books under the Obscene Publications Act.
- The day after the jury delivered its verdict in favour of Penguin, shoppers queued outside bookshops and 200,000 copies were purchased on that first day alone, with 2 million copies being sold in just six weeks.

SUGGESTED COMPANION BOOKS

- *Women in Love* and *The Rainbow* by D. H. LAWRENCE – considered to be the author's two greatest novels.
- *Howards End* by E. M. FORSTER – Forster was a witness in support of *Lady Chatterley's Lover*; this novel also explores themes of class, sexuality and industrialization.
- *The Trial of Lady Chatterley* by C. H. ROLPH – a transcript of the court case, with commentary on contemporary press reaction.

To Kill a Mockingbird

HARPER LEE

Published 1960 / Length 336 pages

'Shoot all the bluejays you want, if you can hit 'em,
but remember it's a sin to kill a mockingbird.'

Set in the fictional town of Maycomb in the Deep South, *To Kill a Mockingbird* tells a compelling tale of innocence and injustice. Our guide is young Jean Louise Finch, known as Scout throughout the novel, who shares with us her personal journey growing up in the 1930s in a small town where corruption and prejudice are rife. Yet against this politically charged backdrop, Scout's father, Atticus, a model of moral guidance, teaches Scout and her brother Jem to understand others and counsels them not to judge people just because they are different. The book's enduring motif of the mockingbird as a symbol of purity and beauty is dramatically enhanced when Atticus, a lawyer, agrees to defend a black man named Tom Robinson, who is accused of raping a white woman. However, the woman in question, Mayella Ewell, comes from a family notorious for lying and stealing. It soon becomes obvious that this court case isn't about justice, but racism. The resulting tensions force many of Maycomb's inhabitants to show their true colours.

READER'S OPINION

'*To Kill a Mockingbird* is an inspiring tale of compassion, loyalty and unfailing love, as a respected small-town lawyer struggles to prove a black man's innocence in a highly racist community. I found it to be a very moving read, highlighting social issues that are still relevant today, despite the fact that the novel is over forty years old.' – MARIANNE, 26

Discussion points

- The persecution of Tom is much more obvious than that of Boo Radley. What purpose does Boo's character serve?

- Lee uses the characters of Heck Tate and Miss Maudie to tell the reader about Atticus. How effective do you think this is?

- Even though Atticus is a morally righteous man, some of his actions are legally ambiguous. Does this change your opinion of him?

- How does the innocence of Scout, as the narrator, affect the way in which the plot is revealed?

- Do you think the issues raised in *To Kill a Mockingbird* are still relevant to modern society?

Background information

- *To Kill a Mockingbird* is the only novel Lee has ever written. It won the 1961 Pulitzer Prize and has since sold over 30 million copies.

- Lee openly acknowledges that the fictional characters in the book are based loosely on her own family and friends, and positions herself as the central character Scout.

Suggested companion books

- *Their Eyes Were Watching God* by Zora Neale Hurston – examines racial abuse.

- *The Lovely Bones* by Alice Sebold (see page 184) – also scrutinizes crime and the community.

- *The Adventures of Huckleberry Finn* by Mark Twain (see page 208) – tackles innocence and racism. Compare the treatment of Jim to that of Tom Robinson; also compare the way in which Scout and Huck behave.

Small Island

Andrea Levy

Published 2004 / Length 530 pages

Small Island tells the story of two couples: Jamaican ex-RAF serviceman Gilbert and his new wife, Hortense, who emigrate to Britain in 1948 hoping for a better life in the Mother Country; and British pair Bernard and Queenie, already living in London. After Bernard fails to return from fighting in the Second World War, Queenie makes ends meet by letting her shabby attic room to Gilbert and snobbish Hortense, who is horrified to find that England is very different to the genteel land of her dreams. Gilbert is distressed, too, as he realizes the English treat him with even more contempt now he's out of uniform. But all this is nothing compared to how bigoted Bernard proves when he finally returns home to discover his house full of 'coloureds'. In this lovingly researched tale of prejudice and ignorance in post-war Britain, Levy uses authentic dialogue and a first-person narrative to place an important part of history under the spotlight. Perhaps what's most impressive is how she manages to portray both black and white experiences of racism with wit, compassion and an even hand.

What the critics said

'The sheer excellence of Levy's research goes beyond the granddad tales of fifty-year-old migrant experience, or the nuts and bolts of historical fact. Her imagination illuminates old stories in a way that almost persuades you she was there at the time.' – *The Guardian*

Discussion points

- To what might the 'small island' of the title refer?
- Why do you think the author chose to tell the story from four different viewpoints? How successful was this?

- Bernard is a blinkered racist, yet his views are given as much importance as those of the other characters. What do you think the author was trying to achieve by showing events through his eyes?
- Reviewers have praised the book as 'a wonderful insight into a little-understood period'. Do you agree? If at all, how has the book altered your perceptions of post-war Britain?
- Think about the characters' situation at the end of the novel. Did anything surprise you about the ending? What do you imagine happens next?

BACKGROUND INFORMATION

- *Small Island* won the 2004 Orange Prize for Fiction, the 2004 Whitbread Novel Award, and the 2005 Commonwealth Writer's Prize for Best Book.
- Levy is a British-born child of Jamaican parents who came to London following the Second World War. Many of Levy's mother's experiences were used in the book.

SUGGESTED COMPANION BOOKS

- *White Teeth* by ZADIE SMITH – Smith's tale of three immigrant families has been praised by Levy as one of the first books to bring black British writing to the bestseller lists.
- *Brick Lane* by MONICA ALI (see page 14) – describes a young Asian woman's culture shock at coming to London from Bangladesh.
- *The Emigrants* by GEORGE LAMMING – on arrival in London, a group of West Indians are disillusioned by the realities of post-war Britain.

Atonement

Ian McEwan

Published 2001 / Length 388 pages

Atonement is a three-part novel, which begins in the country house of the slightly arriviste upper-middle-class Tallis family in 1935. When Briony Tallis, a fanciful, highly imaginative thirteen-year-old, observes her elder sister Cecilia strip and dive into a fountain in front of Robbie Turner, the charlady's son, she mistakenly believes that Cecilia has been forced to perform to satisfy Robbie's lust. This assumption, together with further misconceptions by Briony, lead to disastrous, haunting consequences that shape the rest of the novel. Part two of the book concentrates in graphic detail on Robbie's involvement in the Dunkirk evacuation, perhaps affording a sense of perspective on one foolish child's actions in the context of many atrocities. Part three recounts Briony's career as a nurse in war-ravaged London, dealing with the terrible casualties of battle and facing up to the dreadful repercussions of her childhood errors. McEwan's mastery of the narrative voice, moving from that of a 1930s novel at the start of the book to a modernist, almost stream-of-consciousness style at the end, is a literary tour de force, as well as being a profound meditation on the nature of art, forgiveness, and whether atonement is ever truly possible.

WHAT THE CRITICS SAID

'Reassuringly, even as [*Atonement*] plays postmodern games, it continues to explore many of McEwan's customary interests: the collision between childish whimsy and adult authority, the tyranny of libido, and the conflict between masculine and feminine perspectives. . . . More than ever before, the author is intrigued with the machinery of myth-making, and with the power of narrative to create and manipulate truth.' – *Financial Times*

Discussion points

- On a structural level, the novel is a fascinating exploration of the concept of an unreliable narrator. The book is initially written in the third person, but then shifts to the first as Briony confesses her deception to the reader. What can we, the reader, believe?

- Misconceptions and lies, forms of fiction in themselves, generate the book's central turning points. What does the novel have to say about the act of creating and writing fictions?

- The novel poses a powerful moral question: does Briony's devotion to the victims of war go some way to atoning for her earlier actions? Can the creation of the work of art we are reading also contribute to this atonement?

Background information

- *Atonement* was nominated for the 2001 Booker Prize, which McEwan had previously won in 1998 with his novel *Amsterdam*.

Suggested companion books

- *The French Lieutenant's Woman* by JOHN FOWLES – another time-slipping narrative.

- *A Passage to India* by E. M. FORSTER – an Edwardian novel in which one man's fate turns on the unreliable testimony of a woman, as she alleges sexual impropriety.

- *What Maisie Knew* by HENRY JAMES – an account of divorce within a dysfunctional family, narrated through the eyes of a precocious child, who ages, and whose perspective on events matures, as the novel progresses.

Life of Pi

YANN MARTEL

Published 2002 / Length 319 pages

'I have a story that will make you believe in God.'

Life of Pi is a bold, exciting and energetic novel in which the miraculous seaborne adventures of our intrepid young hero, Piscine Molitor Patel (aka Pi), probe the outer limits of what we are prepared to believe. It is impossible to read this expansive book, the ambitions of which are as wide as Pi's horizon on his little mid-Pacific floating world, without an open mind. The story may defy belief, but the author takes frank pleasure in challenging his reader to take a leap of faith. 'The better story', Pi insists, is the one that is difficult to credit, the one whose imagination and daring fill us with a richer sense of what it is to be alive. For most readers, Pi's fierce optimism, blazing bravely away under that endless sky, proves infectious. Prepare for wicked dashes of humour and anthropomorphism galore. This big-minded little book could just change your life.

READER'S OPINION

'I enjoyed this fantastical tale of tiger-taming in watery extremis as a story told for its own sake, until events moved beyond fiction into an illusion that uncomfortably reframed the earlier narrative, presenting the reader with the challenge that faced Pi himself: the need to believe. Matchless!' – AGATHE, 49

DISCUSSION POINTS

- Do the preface and closing interview that sandwich the story of Pi's odyssey make what he tells us in the middle more or less plausible?
- Martel is adamant that fear is 'life's only true opponent'. How does Pi cope with the fear that his situation produces in him?

- Why has the sea so often been used as a metaphor for the struggle of life itself? Is Pi's voyage a parable for suffering and survival?
- Why do you think Martel chose to structure the book into precisely one hundred chapters – and to point out to the reader that he had done so?

Background information

- The number pi (3.14159 . . .) was made, in mathematicians' early approximations, by dividing 22 by 7; Piscine Molitor Patel spends 227 days in the ocean. Mere coincidence?
- According to Martel, the name Richard Parker alludes to a cabin boy cannibalized by shipwrecked sailors in *The Narrative of Arthur Gordon Pym of Nantucket*, an 1838 novel by horror writer Edgar Allan Poe.
- *Life of Pi* won the 2002 Booker Prize.

Suggested companion books

- *The Master and Margarita* by MIKHAIL BULGAKOV – this Russian magic-realist classic shares much of *Life of Pi*'s imaginative abandon, heart and humanity, and features a memorably voluble feline.
- *Gulliver's Travels* by JONATHAN SWIFT – an eye-opening voyage through incredible unknown worlds, though in this case the author uses the fantastical as a tool to satirize and condemn the political and social realities of eighteenth-century England.

Liars and Saints

Maile Meloy

Published 2003 / Length 260 pages

Liars and Saints is a deceptively simple book – but to read it on a simplistic level alone is to do it an injustice. Chronicling the lives of an American family from the 1940s to the dawn of the new millennium, Meloy's debut novel examines betrayal, anguish and deceit, and sympathetically uncovers the Santerres' efforts to come to terms with all of these. Capturing the tone of each successive generation with accomplished skill, the novel's vast time spectrum features wars abroad and assassinations at home, yet none of these major world events has much lasting effect on the family. Instead, it is the private, domestic sphere of the heart with which Meloy is concerned, and where she brings her most poignant narratives into focus. Underpinning and determining the lives of the family is a committed adherence to Catholicism: transgression and redemption abound, as family secrets are concealed and revealed at breakneck pace. *Liars and Saints* explores the dichotomy between the superficial manner in which people are perceived and the hidden reality of their lives, and what happens when the two collide.

What the critics said

'Although [Meloy] was born and lives in America, her book reads Canadian, with its careful balancing of themes, its compassionate lies, its characters' over-conscientious love and worry and guilt. What you don't get is high drama, or even much in the way of simmering tension.' – *The Guardian*

Discussion points

● It is easy to identify the liars of the title, but are there any saints? What criteria might be used to identify the latter?

- To what extent do you think the main characters' religious background informs their actions? Does it lead any of them to happiness?
- Do you think Jamie's unusual position in the family affected the person he became?
- How far do deceit, guilt and jealousy play a part in events?
- What do you think of the denouement in the final chapters? Is it believable?

BACKGROUND INFORMATION

- *Liars and Saints* was shortlisted for the 2005 Orange Prize for Fiction.
- The novel was a *Richard & Judy* Summer Read choice in 2004.

SUGGESTED COMPANION BOOKS

- *Brideshead Revisited* by EVELYN WAUGH (see page 216) – examines the effect of a Catholic background on a family and their relationships.
- *Brother and Sister* by JOANNA TROLLOPE – explores the importance of finding one's identity through the experiences of two adults adopted in childhood.
- *The Photograph* by PENELOPE LIVELY – describes a man's obsessive interest in an old photograph of his late wife and his efforts to find the 'truth' behind it.
- *A Family Daughter* by MAILE MELOY – another Santerre story focusing on Abby and a different version of events.

Cloud Atlas

DAVID MITCHELL

Published 2004 / Length 529 pages

A novel made up of an ensemble cast of six wildly different stories that fit together, one inside the next like a Russian matrioshka doll, *Cloud Atlas* is a masterful, complex work spanning time and place. The structure in the first half of the book gives the feeling of an upward slope of suspense and set-ups, with each of the stories interrupted, often abruptly, around the halfway point, to be replaced by the next narrative. The pay-off to navigating this series of cliffhangers and half-told tales is the downward slope, where the stories are concluded in reverse order and the reader is able to freewheel gloriously from the denouement of one half-remembered tale to the next, connecting the themes that tie the book together. Each of the narratives is loosely linked to the next in a material sense – for example, the first story, the diary of Adam Ewing, a nineteenth-century American lawyer travelling in the Pacific, is unearthed in 1931 by the protagonist of the next tale, Robert Frobisher, a composer whose genius is quite at odds with his finances. However, there is a strong suggestion throughout that between the central characters of these six stories – stories that run from the past through to a post-apocalyptic future, employing remarkable shifts in style and voice – there exists an underlying and elemental connection.

WHAT THE CRITICS SAID

'*Cloud Atlas* is powerful and elegant because of Mitchell's understanding of the way we respond to those fundamental and primitive stories we tell about good and evil, love and destruction, beginnings and ends. He isn't afraid to jerk tears or ratchet up suspense – he understands that's what we make stories for.' – *The Guardian*

Discussion points

- What themes do you see running through each of *Cloud Atlas*'s six stories? Is there a consistent point of view with regard to these themes?
- What do you think is the relationship between the stories' central characters? What is the significance of the birthmark?
- Robert Frobisher questions whether the structure for his Cloud Atlas Sextet 'for overlapping soloists' is revolutionary or gimmicky. Which best describes *Cloud Atlas* the novel?
- Each of the stories is written in a very specific style, often redolent of a certain genre, if not a specific book. Discuss the various styles employed and how they compare to one another. Which other works do you think are evoked by Mitchell?

Background information

- *Cloud Atlas* was shortlisted for the 2004 Booker Prize and won the 2005 British Book Awards Literary Fiction Award and the *Richard & Judy* Best Read of the Year Award.

Suggested companion books

- *Orlando* by Virginia Woolf – exploring a single life through numerous historical and geographical worlds.
- *If on a Winter's Night a Traveller* by Italo Calvino – Mitchell's inspiration for *Cloud Atlas*: a series of interrupted, varying stories linked through an exploration of similar themes.
- *The Time Traveler's Wife* by Audrey Niffenegger (see page 156) – a love story set against a backdrop of unpredictable time travel.

Beloved

Toni Morrison

Published 1987 / Length 275 pages

'I'll explain to her, even though I don't have to. Why I did it.
How if I hadn't killed her she would have died . . .'

Toni Morrison's masterpiece focuses on the tale of Sethe, a nineteenth-century African-American slave-woman. At the start of the story she is now free, living in Cincinnati, Ohio, with her teenage daughter, Denver. Sethe once had two sons, long vanished, and a baby daughter whom she murdered eighteen years earlier, known only as 'Beloved' (the single word on her tombstone, which Sethe paid for by prostituting herself with the engraver). Now living in an isolated house haunted by the vengeful child's spirit, Sethe is visited by Paul D, a fellow former slave who had worked alongside her at the ironically named Sweet Home Farm in Kentucky. Through a series of conversations and flashbacks, we gradually learn the circumstances that led both characters to their current positions, as well as Sethe's motives for killing her daughter. The narrative circles warily around the traumatic events at the heart of the story – we catch hints and glimpses, but then it wheels off again in another direction before suddenly, horrifically, bringing the incidents into sharp focus. It is an experimental technique that gives the novel a mythical resonance.

WHAT THE CRITICS SAID

'If there were any doubts about [Morrison's] stature as a pre-eminent American novelist, of her own or any other generation, *Beloved* will put them to rest. In three words or less, it's a hair-raiser.' – MARGARET ATWOOD, *The New York Times*

DISCUSSION POINTS

- In the terms of the book – leaving morals aside – did Sethe do the right thing when she killed Beloved? Were the local community right to shun her afterwards?

- 'To love anything that much was dangerous, especially if it was her children' – do you think the story supports Paul D's view? Compare Sethe's view of motherhood.

- Why do you think Morrison tells the story in a fragmented way, juxtaposing past and present? Do you think this impressionistic style undermines the historical accuracy of her depiction of mid-nineteenth-century African-American life?

BACKGROUND INFORMATION

- Sethe's story is loosely based on the life of an escaped slave, Margaret Garner, who in 1856 killed her two-year-old daughter rather than see her returned to slavery.

- The novel won the Pulitzer Prize in Fiction in 1988.

SUGGESTED COMPANION BOOKS

- *The Color Purple* by ALICE WALKER (see page 212) – another harrowing classic of African-American literature.

- *Uncle Tom's Cabin* by HARRIET BEECHER STOWE – 1852 bestseller which helped to alert the world to the evils of slavery, though now dated by its stereotyping.

- *To the Lighthouse* by VIRGINIA WOOLF – an experimental novel with shifting perspectives and time frames. Morrison wrote her master's thesis on the works of Woolf and William Faulkner.

- *Wuthering Heights* by EMILY BRONTË – ambiguous use of the supernatural.

Labyrinth

KATE MOSSE

Published 2005 / Length 694 pages

Kate Mosse's richly imagined historical novel mixes conspiracy, intrigue and adventure through the astonishing narratives of its two central heroines, Alice Tanner and Alaïs Pelletier. Based on thorough research, the book conjures a believable version of thirteenth-century Languedoc, bringing to life the social, political and private lives of Cathars, northern Crusaders and the Inquisition. In the midst of brutal genocide, Alaïs struggles to protect an ancient secret, one that traces back to Egyptian civilization, a secret shrouded in mystery and protected by a shadowy cult. Alongside this narrative strand is a modern-day thriller, sparked when two skeletons are found in a cave during an unusual archaeological dig in southern France. With a plot that spans eight hundred years, *Labyrinth* is an ambitious story, made captivating and gripping by the two immersive worlds created by Mosse. Unlocking the secret of the labyrinth and the identities of the two corpses brings out the novel's profound and moving central conundrum.

WHAT THE CRITICS SAID

'*Labyrinth* is very much a *Girl's Own* story: a grail quest in which women aren't helpless creatures to be rescued, or decorative bystanders, but central to the action, with the capacity to change history.' – *The Observer*

DISCUSSION POINTS

- Strong women abound in this novel, both heroines and villains. Where do you think the novel's emphasis lies, though, on what it takes to be a 'strong woman'?
- In contrast, what do you think of the men in the book –

specifically Will Franklin, Jehan Congost, Guilhem du Mas and Audric Baillard?

- There are many religions and cultures in the book; what do you think the book's principal message is about differences or similarities of faith?

- How successful do you think the dual narrative is? What do the two stories reveal in each other?

- How do more recent acts of genocide, such as the Holocaust, compare to the events described in *Labyrinth*? Do you think the book offers a response to war?

BACKGROUND INFORMATION

- The book was selected as the Best Read of 2006 by the *Richard & Judy* Book Club.

- Kate Mosse co-founded the Orange Prize for Fiction.

- During the research and writing of *Labyrinth*, Mosse set up a website with her husband (www.mosselabyrinth.co.uk), which captured her creative process and built a community around her passion for the history of southern France in the thirteenth century.

- In July 2006, sales of *Labyrinth* in the UK reached 1 million copies.

SUGGESTED COMPANION BOOKS

- *The Name of the Rose* by UMBERTO ECO – a mystery set in a monastery in 1327 Italy, during a similar period of heresy and Inquisition.

- *Fugitive Pieces* by ANNE MICHAELS – a young boy runs from the Nazis, escaping into history and poetry.

- *The Da Vinci Code* by DAN BROWN – an inventive grail-quest conspiracy.

- *Enlightenment* by MAUREEN FREELY – strong women struggle to unlock the truth behind a gruesome murder.

Norwegian Wood

Haruki Murakami

Published 1987 / Length 389 pages

The Beatles song 'Norwegian Wood (This Bird Has Flown)' will always remind Toru Watanabe of Naoko, the girlfriend of his childhood friend, Kisuki, who committed suicide aged seventeen. In this introspective coming-of-age tale, Toru looks back twenty years to his time as a student in Tokyo in the late 1960s. Riddled with comic tales of room-mates, sexual adventure and youthful misadventure, the book at once aches with nostalgia and a beautiful sadness. The adult Toru relates his youthful encounters with the inhibited Naoko, the kooky and sexually liberated Midori, a charming libertine, a dying man and a reclusive middle-aged music teacher. The thriving, packed metropolis of Tokyo forms the setting for most of the book, with a retreat into the mountainous hills beyond Kyoto providing a perfect contrast. This is a thought-provoking and poignant study of memory, morality and mortality; of personal and social responsibility and the expectation of youth; a melancholic exploration of adolescent love and loss, written with a poetic richness that leaves almost every line hanging with symbolic possibility.

What the critics said

'Within this simple, sad love story – a story that deserves to garner Murakami as large a readership as he has in Japan – lives a fascinating cultural portrait of the Summer of Love, Japan-style.' – *Los Angeles Times*

Discussion points

● The narrative is set against a backdrop of student strikes and protests. How does Toru's opinion of these events develop? How does the fact that we know the tale is being told retrospectively affect the portrayal of the student movement?

- Think about the love the characters feel for each other. How do the ways in which they express their love differ? Is anyone being more selfish in their demands for love?
- Where does responsibility lie for what happens to each of the characters? Is anyone to blame? Was Naoko fair to Toru, and he to her?
- How does death affect the lives of those in the novel?

BACKGROUND INFORMATION

- Although evocative of and entirely set in Japan, Murakami wrote *Norwegian Wood* while in Greece and Italy.
- When first published, the book sold more than 4 million copies, making Murakami Japan's biggest-selling novelist and a pop-culture icon. Murakami did not expect or enjoy such superstardom and moved back to Europe. He returned to Japan in 1995, still refusing to court his celebrity.
- A first translation (published 1989) was intended as an English study aid for Japanese students, with grammar notes in the back.

SUGGESTED COMPANION BOOKS

- *In Praise of Older Women* by STEPHEN VIZINCZEY – another coming-of-age tale.
- *The Bell Jar* by SYLVIA PLATH (see page 168) – a semi-autobiographical account of mental breakdown.
- *South of the Border, West of the Sun* by HARUKI MURAKAMI – a bitter-sweet romance.
- *A Wild Sheep Chase* by HARUKI MURAKAMI – a mixed-genre absurdist mystery, typical of Murakami's usual fantastical magical realism.

Top Ten War Books

War, despite or perhaps because of its mindless horrors, is a rich breeding ground for literary inspiration. Here are ten of the best war books, spanning the US Civil War, the Indian Mutiny, the Vietnam War and both the World Wars, with varying perspectives.

The Red Badge of Courage by STEPHEN CRANE

The Siege of Krishnapur by J. G. FARRELL

Strange Meeting by SUSAN HILL

Dispatches by MICHAEL HERR

Schindler's Ark by THOMAS KENEALLY

The Naked and the Dead by NORMAN MAILER

The Cruel Sea by NICHOLAS MONSARRAT

All Quiet on the Western Front
by ERICH MARIA REMARQUE

The Memoirs of George Sherston
by SIEGFRIED SASSOON

A Town Like Alice by NEVIL SHUTE

Top Ten Crime Books

Crime books regularly hold the top spot on the bestseller lists and there is no doubting the popularity of this well-established genre. For page-turning suspense, thrilling plot twists, baffling mysteries and a healthy dose of fear and foreboding, crime novels are second to none. Enjoy these classics by masters in the field.

The Big Sleep by RAYMOND CHANDLER

And Then There Were None by AGATHA CHRISTIE

Cruel and Unusual by PATRICIA CORNWELL

The Devil's Teardrop by JEFFERY DEAVER

The Memoirs of Sherlock Holmes
by ARTHUR CONAN DOYLE

The Black Dahlia by JAMES ELLROY

The Maltese Falcon by DASHIELL HAMMETT

A Taste for Death by P. D. JAMES

Motherless Brooklyn by JONATHAN LETHEM

A Fatal Inversion by RUTH RENDELL

The Sea, The Sea

IRIS MURDOCH

Published 1978 / Length 538 pages

The title of this classic novel by Iris Murdoch refers to the ancient Greeks' cry at the end of the 'march of the ten thousand', when from atop Mount Theches they suddenly spy the glimmering sea in the distance. In such a spirit of hope does the central character of the book, one Charles Arrowby, former tyrannical theatre star, arrive at his own promised land by the sea: a peculiar, possibly haunted house called Shruff End, set on a deserted stretch of English shore. But as Charles fantasizes that he can escape his former life and thoughts, some come knocking unwanted, some he summons to him, and one he unexpectedly comes across in the village, appearing to him as an apparition from the past. Then James, his cousin and rival, arrives, and events take an ugly, murderous turn . . . Interweaved through the book are endless beautiful descriptions of the ever-present sea.

WHAT THE CRITICS SAID

'Arrowby . . . is a typical Murdoch creation, a compelling, fully realized character and at the same time a symbolic, Prospero-like figure who will explore the many ideas that Murdoch introduces into her narrative . . . The recognition of the value of the imperfect is a constant theme in Murdoch's work, and *The Sea, The Sea* expresses a central part of her philosophy with astounding vigour and characteristic imaginative clarity.' – *The Observer*

DISCUSSION POINTS

- Pervading the book is the wish to withdraw, to gain enlightenment through pure reflection. How serious do you think Charles's various attempts at purity are?
- Do you find Charles as a central character likeable in certain

ways, or is he ultimately selfish? Do you find him misogynistic? How does this affect your enjoyment of the book?

- Do the various 'almost recipes' through the book affect your reading of it? Do you take away anything from Charles's description of the 'precious gift' of hunger?

- The book often attempts to speak to the inner mind, for example: 'I thought, I must be ingenious, and the word "ingenious" seemed like a help to me. I must be ingenious and see to it that I do not suffer too much. I must look for some happiness, simply for some comfort, here, ingeniously.' Do such attempts resonate with you?

BACKGROUND INFORMATION

- *The Sea, The Sea* won the 1978 Booker Prize and was one of the most successful of Iris Murdoch's twenty-six novels, all of which have earned her acclaim as one of the English language's greatest novelists of recent years.

- As well as writing novels, Murdoch was a fellow of Oxford University, where she taught philosophy. Before her death in 1999, she suffered from Alzheimer's disease. Her husband, novelist John Bayley, wrote a memoir of their life together, *Iris* (1999), which was made into an Academy Award-winning film in 2001, starring Judi Dench and Kate Winslet as Murdoch.

SUGGESTED COMPANION BOOKS

- *Offshore* by PENELOPE FITZGERALD – another tale of life by the water, and winner of the Booker Prize in the following year, 1979.

- *Holiday* by STANLEY MIDDLETON – a story of marriages, deaths, shattered lives and reunited loves in an English seaside town.

- *The Tempest* by WILLIAM SHAKESPEARE – *The Sea, The Sea* has strong echoes of this play.

Lolita

Vladimir Nabokov

Published 1955 / Length 368 pages

An extraordinary masterpiece of subtle horror, *Lolita* was one of the most controversial novels of the twentieth century. The evasive and ingratiating narrative voice is that of Humbert Humbert, intellectual and monster, who is fixated on the sexual pursuit of young girls: nymphets or 'demon children', as he terms them. The events of the novel are filtered through the prism of Humbert's dazzling prose, as he mounts an impassioned and erudite defence of his depravity. Leaving his native Europe for America after spells in various facilities of psychological correction, Humbert becomes the lodger of Charlotte Haze, a suburban widow with a twelve-year-old daughter – Dolores, Lo, Dolly or Lolita – with whom Humbert becomes dangerously obsessed. It's a challenging read – Nabokov's beautifully wrought prose resonates with literary and cultural references and deft wordplay – that has lost none of its power to shock.

What the critics said

'The filthiest book I have ever read . . . sheer, unrestrained pornography.' – *Sunday Express*, 1955

Discussion points

- Does any responsibility for the novel's events lie with Lolita? Does she ever have control of the plot or of Humbert?
- In what ways does Nabokov lead us to distrust Humbert's narration?
- *Lolita* is peppered with comedy, albeit often tragicomedy. Is it possible to enjoy Humbert's puns and barbed wit in the context of the novel's disturbing subject matter?
- The book has been interpreted as a metaphor, casting

Humbert as Old Europe – cultured but corrupt – and Lolita as America – 'ripening, beautiful, but not too bright and a little vulgar', in the words of critic Simon Leake. Does this reading work?

● What roles are played by fate and coincidence in the novel?

BACKGROUND INFORMATION

● Four American publishers rejected *Lolita* due to the subject matter, but it was eventually published in Paris. British Customs seized imported copies and it was subsequently banned in France for two years.

● The first American edition in 1958 sold 100,000 copies in the first three weeks of publication.

● *Lolita* has been filmed twice: in 1962 by Stanley Kubrick, starring James Mason, and in 1997 by Adrian Lyne, starring Jeremy Irons. In both cases, the actresses playing Lolita appeared older than she actually is at the beginning of the book – she is only twelve years old when Humbert first meets her.

● In Brian Boyd's biography of Nabokov, *Vladimir Nabokov: The American Years* (1991), he details the author's intensive research for *Lolita*: 'He would do things like travel on the buses around Ithaca, New York and record phrases, in a little notebook, from young girls that he heard coming back from school.' As a European writing about 1950s America, Nabokov felt it was crucial to make these nuances ring true.

SUGGESTED COMPANION BOOKS

● *Reading Lolita in Tehran* by AZAR NAFISI – a covert Iranian women's book group discuss banned Western literature, including *Lolita*.

● *Oryx and Crake* by MARGARET ATWOOD – a futuristic portrait of a sexually precocious young girl.

Suite Française

Irène Némirovsky

Published 2004 / Length 342 pages

First conceived as a series of five segments, *Suite Française* comprises the two surviving sections of a book written by Irène Némirovsky in 1941–2 during the German occupation of France, just before her death in a concentration camp in 1942. The manuscript was kept by her daughter and rediscovered in 2004, when it received great acclaim for its portrayal of ordinary people coping with extraordinary events.

The first section, 'Storm in June', is set in 1940 as Parisians flee their city to avoid the Germans' approach. The characters come from very different backgrounds and, despite their chaotic and desperate circumstances, they cannot overcome class barriers to work together. 'Dolce', the second section, is set under the Occupation a year later, as villagers struggle to share houses and break bread with those who may have harmed their loved ones. At once heartbreaking and shockingly straightforward, the book captures the resilience of the human spirit.

READER'S OPINION

'What I really enjoyed was all the small details. It's true: the country might be at war, but you don't forget stupid things like the time your neighbour wouldn't let you have an egg.'
– EVELYN, 77

DISCUSSION POINTS

- 'Suite' can mean a group of rooms. Is this how we should see the two segments – as adjacent but essentially separate?
- How does the context (the background information about the circumstances in which the book was written) affect your reading of the book?

- 'What separates or unites people is not their language, their laws, their customs, but the way they hold their knife and fork.' Does the novel prove or disprove Viscountess de Montmort's theory?

BACKGROUND INFORMATION

- Némirovsky wrote nine novels, including *David Golber* (1929). These established her as a successful writer and her name became well known across Europe in her lifetime.
- Némirovsky was born into a wealthy Russian-Jewish family in 1903, but fled the country for France in 1918 after the Revolution. Her family lost most of their wealth during this time, but soon re-established themselves in Paris at the heart of upper-class society. Despite being persecuted by the Nazis for being Jewish, Némirovsky never practised any religion, openly socialized with anti-Semitic people and even converted to Catholicism in 1939, perhaps hoping to avoid detection.
- *Suite Française* won one of France's top literary prizes, the Prix Renaudot, in 2004.

SUGGESTED COMPANION BOOKS

- *The Diary of a Young Girl* by ANNE FRANK – another 'found' manuscript written while the author was hiding from the Nazis.
- *If This Is a Man* by PRIMO LEVI – describes life inside a concentration camp in an astute manner that echoes Némirovsky's work.
- *A Woman in Berlin*, published anonymously – an intelligent, cultured woman's account of the terrible summer of 1945 in Berlin.

The Time Traveler's Wife

AUDREY NIFFENEGGER
Published 2004 / Length 518 pages

The Time Traveler's Wife is a beautifully written, totally original love story. Despite its title, it is not rooted in science fiction, but rather in its protagonists' lifelong romance. Henry and Clare met when Clare was six and Henry thirty-six, and married when Clare was twenty-two and Henry thirty. The reason for this skewed chronology is that Henry suffers from so-called 'chrono-displacement disorder', a condition whereby he time travels: without warning, he leaves his present and arrives in the past or future. Through this uncertainty comes one truth: his love for Clare, and hers for him, as she waits time and time again for him to return to her. While their situation is extraordinary, the evolution of their relationship is strikingly universal: their joys, hopes and fears are hauntingly familiar and poignantly evoked. It is a story of soulmates; an intelligent foray into fate and determinism; a convincingly written book that lifts the spirits, even as its ominous undertones threaten to overwhelm both the characters and the reader.

WHAT THE CRITICS SAID

'How should we read Henry's slips and tumbles through time? As a metaphor for addiction or recurrent illness; a symbol of imagination taking flight; or a woman writer's sly parable about the eternally absent nature of men?' – *The Independent*

DISCUSSION POINTS

- The title places Clare as the eponymous character – yet defined only in terms of her relationship to Henry. Do you think this accurately reflects Clare's character throughout the book?

- Think about the different responses to grief in the book. How does loss inform who the characters eventually become?
- Why do you think Niffenegger chose to tell the story from both Henry's and Clare's viewpoints? How successful is she in capturing their fluctuating ages?
- The book raises questions of free will and determinism. Can Henry and Clare do anything to change their fate? Can any of us?
- Is time-travelling ultimately seen as a blessing or a curse?

BACKGROUND INFORMATION

- *The Time Traveler's Wife* started life as a title. It took four and a half years to complete.
- Niffenegger is an American art professor who has written and published her own visual-art books since she was a teenager. This is her first traditional novel.
- The book was selected for the *Richard & Judy* Book Club and won the Popular Fiction prize at the 2006 British Book Awards.

SUGGESTED COMPANION BOOKS

- *Wuthering Heights* by EMILY BRONTË – depicts two lovers tied to each other through adversity; and disparate reactions to, and the long-term impact of, grief.
- *Pygmalion* by GEORGE BERNARD SHAW – this play examines the influence of an older man on a younger woman. Does Henry mould Clare in a similar way?
- *Woman on the Edge of Time* by MARGE PIERCY (see page 164) – another time-travel narrative scrutinizing free will and determinism.

Nineteen Eighty-Four

GEORGE ORWELL

Published 1949 / Length 311 pages

The year is 1984, the setting Oceania; society is controlled by the Party, led by the godlike Big Brother. The increasingly disillusioned protagonist, Winston Smith, begins writing a diary (a crime, as free thought is banned). Soon afterwards, he is approached by Julia, whom he suspects may be a kindred spirit. But in this authoritarian world, deciding whom to trust is fraught with danger. Dare Winston risk all in pursuit of barely imagined freedom? Heavy with symbolism and warning, yet lucid and accessible, Orwell's gripping dystopian tale of rebellion, love, fear and political control is recognized as one of the most influential books ever written.

WHAT THE CRITICS SAID

'*Nineteen Eighty-Four* is a work of pure horror . . . a society which has as its single aim the total destruction of the individual identity . . . [It is] the most contemporary novel of this year and who knows of how many past and to come.' – *The Times*, 1949

DISCUSSION POINTS

- The year 1984 has been and gone – is the novel still relevant today as a vision of a dystopian future? How much of what Orwell warned about has come true?

- When the book was written, the Second World War had recently ended, and Britain was aware of how close it had come to totalitarian rule under the Nazis. What impact does this context have on your reading of *Nineteen Eighty-Four*? What do you think Orwell's main intention was in writing it?

- Think about what attracts Winston to Julia. What are the similarities and differences between them?

- Themes of love and sex feature prominently. Why do you think Orwell felt they were so important?
- Winston believes: 'If there is hope, it lies with the proles.' By the end of the novel, is there any hope left for the citizens of Oceania?

BACKGROUND INFORMATION

- Originally called *The Last Man in Europe*, the title was changed to make the book more marketable. It's not known why Orwell chose *Nineteen Eighty-Four*; it's thought he may have just switched the last two figures of the year in which the book was written: 1948.
- Orwell died seven months after *Nineteen Eighty-Four* was published. One year after publication, it had sold nearly half a million copies. It has since been translated into over sixty languages, and adapted for cinema, television, radio and theatre.
- Phrases from the book that have crossed over into common usage include 'Room 101', 'Newspeak', 'Thought Police' and 'Big Brother'.

SUGGESTED COMPANION BOOKS

- *Brave New World* by ALDOUS HUXLEY (see page 114) – a sci-fi classic that also imagines a future where the public is subconsciously controlled by a ruling elite.
- *The Handmaid's Tale* by MARGARET ATWOOD (see page 20) – explores from a female perspective similar themes of repression and radical government in the not-too-distant future.
- *We* by YEVGENY ZAMYATIN – Orwell acknowledged that this 1920s Russian science-fiction novel about a future dystopia was a huge influence on *Nineteen Eighty-Four*.

Bel Canto

ANN PATCHETT

Published 2001 / Length 318 pages

Mr Hosokawa, an influential business leader, reluctantly attends a presidential party in his honour in an unnamed Latin American country – agreeing to do so only because his favourite opera singer has been booked to perform for him. After Roxane Coss's last song, the lights go out and strangers storm the party in search of the President, whom they mean to kidnap. But the President isn't there. Their rapid in-out operation turns into a prolonged siege. Through close studies of the characters involved, Patchett delineates superbly the anatomy of the siege situation, showing how people and relationships evolve when they are forced to act collectively. Character is exposed. Friendships develop. Love comes to call. But in the streets outside, so far away from this strange temporary utopia, the authorities are moving inexorably to force the siege to its inevitable end.

READER'S OPINION

'I really felt that I could relate to so many characters, because they were so sympathetically drawn. I was completely taken with this novel.'– JANET, 45

DISCUSSION POINTS

- Can a novel like this alter the way in which we judge events in the real world – for instance, the Beslan school tragedy? Or should the siege in *Bel Canto* be viewed merely as a literary device used to bring together a disparate group of characters?

- The book begins with two epigraphs, which enhance our appreciation of the novel as a whole. One of them is unattributed: it is from the libretto for Mozart's opera

The Magic Flute. In what ways do these epigraphs relate to the main body of the story?

- Patchett introduces many different characters and narrative perspectives. Given this, how successful is she in sustaining the pace of the plot?

- How does Patchett coax the reader into questioning or even undoing normative judgements about 'the authorities' versus 'terrorists'? How well does she achieve this?

BACKGROUND INFORMATION

- Patchett based her fiction on fact. In Peru, a few years before *Bel Canto*'s publication, a siege lasted for months when terrorists took hostage 400 people in an ambassadorial house.

- '*Bel canto*', 'beautiful singing' in Italian, is a vocal style with full operatic tones that requires a versatile or even a virtuoso technique.

- In 2002, *Bel Canto* won both the Orange Prize for Fiction and the PEN/Faulkner Award.

SUGGESTED COMPANION BOOKS

- *Music & Silence* by ROSE TREMAIN and *An Equal Music* by VIKRAM SETH – beautiful storytelling with musical themes.

- *The Good Terrorist* by DORIS LESSING – shifting narrative perspectives and a challenge to readers' perceptions.

- *The Feast of the Goat* by MARIO VARGAS LLOSA – a magnificent, multi-voiced work with one narrative line focusing on a group of assassins, which also takes place in Latin America.

- *Terrorist* by JOHN UPDIKE – a more recent example of a writer trying to understand somebody else's utterly alien point of view.

The Pact

JODI PICOULT

Published 1998 / Length 517 pages

The Pact is an emotional and sobering book, which highlights magnificently how adversity can test to the limits even the strongest of friendships and the loyalties we have to others. Chris Harte and Emily Gold have lived next door to each other all their lives. Their two families have shared everything and, at the opening of this book, the Hartes and the Golds are about to share a nightmare. A midnight call shatters their complacency: Emily is dead at seventeen in an apparent suicide pact made with Chris. Picoult plays with emotions very skilfully, skipping from her portrayal of the all-American, perfect, middle-class lifestyle to the awful reality that dawns when tragedy strikes and families are torn apart. The narrative weaves through the mundanity of everyday life, as well as the high drama of a climax-building trial, showing a unique depth of compassion. It is heart-rending in its depiction of the love and sacrifice of one person for another.

READER'S OPINION

'An emotional roller coaster, this book had me empathizing with each of the main characters, but I also grew extremely frustrated with them. "Just let go of your fears and see what's really going on," I wanted to shout at them on more than one occasion.' – HELEN, 30

DISCUSSION POINTS

- Do you think that the parents' reactions are justified? How easy is it to sympathize with them?
- The novel raises a number of moral dilemmas. How successfully does it deal with them? What would you have done in the same scenarios?

- On its cover, the book poses the question, 'Can we ever really know our children?' Another could be, 'Should we stand by them whatever they do?' Discuss.
- Does this novel give a positive or negative assessment of the institution of family?

BACKGROUND INFORMATION

- While still a student of creative writing at Princeton University, Picoult had two of her short stories published in *Seventeen* magazine.
- Picoult's writing deals with love, family and relationships, and is inspired by a happy upbringing and marriage. Since 1992, she has written over a dozen novels, *The Pact* being her fifth.
- In 2002, the book was adapted by Will Scheffer as a made-for-cable-television movie, starring Megan Mullally and Juliet Stevenson.

SUGGESTED COMPANION BOOKS

- *My Best Friend's Girl* by DOROTHY KOOMSON – best friends torn apart by betrayal are brought back together by tragedy.
- *The Island* by VICTORIA HISLOP – a woman's journey to find out the truth about her mother's past.
- *The Outsiders* by S. E. HINTON – two weeks in the life of fourteen-year-old Ponyboy Curtis, who's always known what to expect – until now.
- *We Need to Talk About Kevin* by LIONEL SHRIVER (see page 190) – another troubled teenager tests his mother's loyalty and causes her to question his true nature.

Woman on the Edge of Time

MARGE PIERCY

Published 1976 / Length 381 pages

A time-travel story examining issues of social justice, *Woman on the Edge of Time* is a fierce indictment of the inequality of modern life, an uplifting exploration of what could be, and an audacious call to arms. Connie Ramos is thirty-seven, Mexican-American, poor, female, an inmate of a mental asylum, and a supposed child abuser: a woman undoubtedly on the edge of her 1970s society. Yet Connie is also the eponymous woman on the edge of time, a talented 'catcher' with the ability to communicate telepathically with Luciente – a time traveller from the year 2137 and the future village of Mattapoisett – and to visit Luciente's world, a utopian society in which there is no oppression: no sexism, no racism, no class divides. However, this blissful vision may yet be just that, for there is no guarantee this future will come to pass. Its existence is reliant on Mattapoisett's ancestors – on people like Connie. As the modern world continues its persecution of our heroine, with a horrifying objective in mind, Connie must decide whether or not it's a future worth fighting for.

WHAT THE CRITICS SAID

'What makes *Woman on the Edge of Time* so powerful is the presentation of a utopia alongside a realistic portrayal of contemporary life. For Connie's life in the twentieth century is not science fictional. . . . The comparison illumines the horrors of the present day as well as the liberating potentialities of the future.' – SARAH LEFANU, *In the Chinks of the World Machine* (1988)

DISCUSSION POINTS

● Would you like to live in Mattapoisett? What are its strengths and weaknesses?

- Do you think Piercy exaggerates the position of the powerless in society, and the direction in which such imbalanced civilizations might go?

- What changes would have to occur in the modern world for a society such as Mattapoisett to exist? Do you think we're currently closer to Gildina's culture?

- Do you agree with Luciente's assertion that women 'had to give up . . . the only power [they] ever had, in return for no more power for anyone'? Is this the only way to achieve true equality?

- Were you wholly sympathetic to Connie, or did you ever think that she deserved to be in hospital, that she *was* sick? Do you believe her time-travelling experiences, or is it all just fantasy? Is she right to take the action she does?

BACKGROUND INFORMATION

- Marge Piercy is an American poet, novelist and social activist. Her works include the poetry collection *The Moon Is Always Female*, a feminist classic, and the novel *Body of Glass*, which won the 1993 Arthur C. Clarke Award.

- A utopia is 'an imagined place or state of things in which everything is perfect' (*Oxford Dictionary of English*), from the Greek for 'no place' or 'place that does not exist'. The writer Thomas More was the first to use it in this context, in his 1516 work *Utopia*.

SUGGESTED COMPANION BOOKS

- *Herland* (1915) by Charlotte Perkins Gilman – an early example of feminist utopian fiction.

- *The Time Traveler's Wife* by Audrey Niffenegger (see page 156) – another time-travelling story that poses questions of free will and determinism.

- *One Flew Over the Cuckoo's Nest* by Ken Kesey – also set on a mental ward, this novel explores the effects of the regime on the patients.

Vernon God Little

D. B. C. Pierre

Published 2003 / Length 277 pages

The tour de force that is *Vernon God Little* was indisputably the darkest black comedy to hit the bookshops in 2003. In Martirio, Texas, fifteen-year-old Vernon is wrongly accused of being one of the shooters in a massacre at his local high school. From this moment on, his life (which wasn't perfect in the first place) takes a decidedly catastrophic turn for the worse. Satirizing all of America's nastiest tics, from reality TV and fast-food outlets to the disturbingly deathly justice system, Vernon's story is peopled by some of the funniest, most grotesque, panty-sniffing over-eaters this side of hell. A coming-of-age novel, a political novel, an on-the-road novel, D. B. C. Pierre's book not only defies genres, but also grabs you by the throat from its opening sentence, with language that kicks, gobs and spits off the page, enthralling and appalling to the very last word.

WHAT THE CRITICS SAID

'Read *Vernon God Little* not only for its dangerous relevance, but for the coruscating wit and raw vitality of its voice, which recalls maybe Flannery O'Connor on an overdose of amphetamines and cable television.' – *The List*

DISCUSSION POINTS

- Vernon Gregory Little's authorial voice is not only full of linguistic energy, but it is also highly inventive and at times extremely idiomatic. Does this prejudice the clarity of the story?

- By any stretch of the imagination Vernon Gregory Little isn't a run-of-the-mill central character, but does his irreverence undermine his position as the book's hero?

- The subtitle of the novel is 'A Twenty-First-Century Comedy in the Presence of Death'. What does the story tell us about America at the start of the new century? Is the author's criticism of the USA justified?
- How did the ending of the book strike you? Critics have said that it could be read in two different ways. Do you agree?

BACKGROUND INFORMATION

- The author was born Peter Warren Finlay in Australia. The 'D. B. C' part of Pierre's name supposedly stands for 'Dirty But Clean'.
- In 2003, *Vernon God Little* won the Booker Prize, the Bollinger Everyman Wodehouse Award for Comic Writer and the Whitbread Best First Novel Award.

SUGGESTED COMPANION BOOKS

- *The Catcher in the Rye* by J. D. SALINGER (see page 180) – this classic set the benchmark for coming-of-age novels.
- *Trainspotting* by IRVINE WELSH – does the language in which Welsh tells his story aid or alienate the reader?
- *Morvern Callar* by ALAN WARNER – with an amoral, distinctly bizarre heroine at the heart of this book, how does Morvern's story compare with Vernon's?
- *Sheepshagger* by NIALL GRIFFITHS – as irreverent as it is unsentimental, this novel is wired into the Welsh countryside as much as Vernon's story is wired into the badlands of Texas. How do the very different geographical settings affect the books' characters?

The Bell Jar

SYLVIA PLATH

Published 1963 / Length 258 pages

Esther Greenwood is an all-American, straight-A student, her life ahead seemingly planned out to the last detail. As the novel opens, she is in New York, having won a prestigious contest to work there for a month. She is supposed to be steering the city 'like her own private car. Only [Esther isn't] steering anything, not even [herself].' This semi-autobiographical tale of a 1950s teenager's breakdown has lost none of its power over the decades. With characteristically brilliant imagery, Plath vividly evokes Esther's psychological journey, tracing both the experiences that led to her condition and her mental collapse. A feminist classic that puts women's roles firmly under the spotlight, *The Bell Jar* is a compelling book that scrutinizes social pressures, mother–daughter relationships, sexual hypocrisy and the constructs of femininity.

WHAT THE CRITICS SAID

'No writer exposed the self *in extremis* more eloquently but frighteningly than Sylvia Plath. Her novel . . . was so close to tormented autobiography that it was first published under a pseudonym.' – *The Guardian*

DISCUSSION POINTS

● Plath once wrote to her mother: 'Perhaps I am destined to be classified and qualified. But, oh, I cry out against it' (*Letters Home*, 1975). How does *The Bell Jar* suggest that 1950s society pigeonholes women into limited, mutually exclusive roles? Does this remain a dilemma for women today?

● Is Esther self-aware, or self-deceiving? When do we, as readers, realize she's mad – or isn't she?

- 'Joan was the beaming double of my old best self.' How do the other characters illuminate Esther's position, and her choices? Why do you think Plath gives Joan the fate she does?
- *The Bell Jar* is semi-autobiographical. Can you tell? If so, does it detract from the story or empower it? *The Observer* said that the book 'gains its considerable power from an objectivity that is extraordinary'. Do you agree that Plath is objective?
- By the end, has Esther defeated her demons or been subsumed by them? What were they in the first place?

BACKGROUND INFORMATION

- Plath was a celebrated American poet who posthumously won the 1982 Pulitzer Prize in Poetry for her *Collected Poems*. *The Bell Jar* was her only novel.
- The book is a fictionalized account of Plath's own breakdown as an adolescent: she tried to kill herself in August 1953, having become depressed after failing to make it into a summer-school class at Harvard. Almost ten years later, on 11 February 1963, she committed suicide.
- The novel was first published in Britain in January 1963 under the pseudonym Victoria Lucas. It went on to spend twenty-four weeks on *The New York Times* bestseller list.

SUGGESTED COMPANION BOOKS

- *The Catcher in the Rye* by J. D. SALINGER (see page 180) – another 1950s adolescent breakdown, this time told from a male perspective.
- *Girl, Interrupted* by SUSANNA KAYSEN – an autobiographical account of the author's treatment in a psychiatric hospital in 1967; Kaysen was treated at the same clinic as Plath.
- *Prozac Nation* by ELIZABETH WURTZEL – a less poetic account of mental illness, published in 1994.

Housekeeping

MARILYNNE ROBINSON

Published 1980 / Length 224 pages

In this lyrical first novel, desolation haunts the lakes, mountains and forests of north-west America's 'outsized landscape'. Fingerbone, Idaho is the atmospheric fictional town at the heart of the story, reflecting the author's passion for the natural world. It is here that the narrator Ruth and her younger sister Lucille are abandoned by their mother, who leaves them at their grandmother's house before driving to the lake where her own father drowned. So begins a series of movingly described losses that fill the novel. Robinson portrays contrasting approaches to housekeeping, from the meticulous grandmother to the eccentric aunt, Sylvie. The girls must decide whether to break free from Sylvie's eccentricities and follow convention or pursue a nomadic existence, atypical for women. *Housekeeping* is not only about keeping physical surfaces clean, but also about the depths: how best to tend the spiritual home. This is a novel about the possibilities of survival and self-sufficiency; about the transience of all things, even those we most love.

WHAT THE CRITICS SAID

'Marilynne Robinson has written a first novel that one reads as slowly as poetry – and for the same reason: the language is so precise, so distilled, so beautiful that one doesn't want to miss any pleasure it might yield up to patience.' – *The New York Times*

DISCUSSION POINTS

- The characters approach housekeeping in different ways: what is the wider significance of the varying manners in which they look after their homes?

- The lake is in one sense a symbol of death. In the novel, is the natural environment something to be feared entirely? What other effects does the author achieve through her depiction of the natural world?

- The book presents three generations of women: the grandmother, aunts and nieces. How are their attitudes similar and different?

- What roles do men play in this novel?

- To what extent, if any, do you think Robinson is making a feminist statement?

BACKGROUND INFORMATION

- The novel was awarded the 1981 Hemingway Foundation/ PEN Award for Best First Novel and nominated for the 1982 Pulitzer Prize in Fiction, which Robinson won with her second book, *Gilead*, in 2005.

- A film version of *Housekeeping* was released in 1987, shot in and around British Columbia, directed by Bill Forsyth.

- In 2003, *The Observer* named *Housekeeping* as one of the 100 greatest novels of all time.

SUGGESTED COMPANION BOOKS

- *The Death of Adam: Essays on Modern Thought* by MARILYNNE ROBINSON – this critically acclaimed essay collection examines many of the same themes as *Housekeeping*, including wilderness and civilization.

- *Gilead* by MARILYNNE ROBINSON – the author's Pulitzer Prize-winning second novel contains her familiar concerns of mortality, religion and the gulf between generations.

- *Beloved* by TONI MORRISON (see page 142) – written in a similarly intense lyrical style, Morrison's masterpiece explores fraught family relationships.

The Human Stain

Philip Roth

Published 2000 / Length 361 pages

Coleman Silk, an ageing, well-respected Classics professor at a New England university, is the protagonist of *The Human Stain*; an accusation of racism, leading to his catastrophic fall from grace, sets in motion the novel's compelling and implacable narrative. Brimming over with rage at the senselessness of the charge, the disloyalty of friends and the fatal consequences the scandal has for his wife, Silk resigns his post. In the vacuum that ensues, he stumbles into the life of his reclusive neighbour, Nathan Zuckerman, and demands that Zuckerman, a writer, commit Silk's story to paper. The tale takes an unexpected turn when Silk embarks on a relationship with a local dairy worker, Faunia Farley, whom life has treated with equal disdain. Aided by Viagra, Silk's world is energized by their partnership. However, Farley's deranged Vietnam vet ex-husband, Les, a man consumed by a fury fuelled by witnessing the horrors of war, struggles to deal with his former wife's affair and life outside the army.

Set against the backdrop of Bill Clinton's impeachment for his Oval Office misdeameanours that to some extent is echoed by Silk's own public humiliation, *The Human Stain* is an aggressive, sensual, richly powerful and unapologetic novel. It explores the complexities of secrecy and family history (for Silk has several secrets of his own), questions of identity and self-presentation, and the danger and hypocrisy of moral rectitude.

WHAT THE CRITICS SAID

'A stunning, complex novel of snarling rage, passion, sarcasm, scorching humour and extraordinary beauty.' – *The Observer*

DISCUSSION POINTS

- Some readers consider *The Human Stain* to be a 'masculine' novel, both in its subject material as well as stylistically. Do you agree?

- Roth's portrayal of Silk, Les Farley and Faunia Farley is at times brutal, and rarely unambiguous, but still our sympathies shift. At the close of the novel, with whom do you sympathize, and why?

- In what way is Roth's claim of America's 'ecstasy of sanctimony' a driving factor of the book?

- What is 'the human stain' of the title, and how does the novel suggest its existence?

BACKGROUND INFORMATION

- *The Human Stain* is the last novel in a loosely connected trilogy (see SUGGESTED COMPANION BOOKS), the main unifying element being the character of Nathan Zuckerman, who, it has been claimed, is Roth's alter ego.

- Published to great critical acclaim, the novel won both the PEN/Faulkner Award in the US and the Prix Médicis Étranger in France.

- In 2003, *The Human Stain* was made into a feature film. Silk was played by Anthony Hopkins, Faunia Farley by Nicole Kidman, Les Farley by Ed Harris and Zuckerman by Gary Sinise.

SUGGESTED COMPANION BOOKS

- *American Pastoral* (1997) and *I Married a Communist* (1998) by PHILIP ROTH – the first two books of the 'trilogy' that is concluded by *The Human Stain*.

- *Disgrace* by J. M. COETZEE – also tells the story of a shamed and discredited college professor.

The God of Small Things

ARUNDHATI ROY

Published 1997 / Length 350 pages

Roy's semi-autobiographical first novel begins with Rahel's return to her childhood home in Ayemenem, India, and her reunion with her fraternal 'two-egg' twin, Estha. The narrative structure is intricately wrought, quivering back and forth from past to present, piecing childhood memories together with their future implications with subtlety and inventiveness. Evoking Kerala life with colour and humour, the novel deals with communism, Christianity and the caste system. Parts of the story are filtered through the eyes of a child, recounting the dramatic events of Rahel's childhood and the way in which the horror of an unexpected death has resounded at the heart of her family ever since. A poetic account of pickles, passion, scandal and *The Sound of Music*, *The God of Small Things* is a touching portrayal of how seemingly insignificant incidents can trigger the deepest of emotions.

WHAT THE CRITICS SAID

'What is most admirable about *The God of Small Things* is Roy's attempt to invent her own idiom, to be first with a new way of writing about modern life. There is a powerful sense of language being mangled, stretched and distorted. She has an acute sensitivity to the natural world, filling her pages with smells and sounds, colour and light, with the "small things" of life that are so easily devoured by habitualism.' – *The Times*

DISCUSSION POINTS

● What do you think is the significance of 'the god of small things'? How does the dual perspective of child and adult help to evoke this?

- Roy studied architecture before becoming a novelist. Is it possible to detect this in her style of writing? How would you describe the structure of the narrative in terms of a building?

- The novel has received criticism for its story, while the portrayal of the family is praised as convincing and poignant. Do you agree with the critics? If so, in what way might the fact that the book is semi-autobiographical have influenced this?

BACKGROUND INFORMATION

- The novel won the Booker Prize in 1997.
- Completed in 1996, the book took four years to write.
- Roy received half a million pounds in advances, and rights to the book were sold in twenty-one countries.
- The author has not written anything else to date, concentrating instead on political activism, including campaigning against the Narmada Dam Project in Gujarat.

SUGGESTED COMPANION BOOKS

- *Shame* by SALMAN RUSHDIE – comparable complex writing style in a novel that deals with a Pakistani upbringing.
- *Things Fall Apart* by CHINUA ACHEBE (see page 10) – concerned with the theme of multiple religions and the merging of cultures.
- *The Guide* by R. K. NARAYAN – a book centred on Indian culture, which includes an evocative description of childhood.
- *Atonement* by IAN MCEWAN (see page 134) – has a similarly elliptical narrative structure that shifts temporally.

Top Ten Gay Reads

Critical acclaim has surrounded recent gay novels such as the Booker Prize-winning *The Line of Beauty* and Sarah Waters's entire body of work. Here are ten classics of gay literature.

Giovanni's Room by JAMES BALDWIN

Don Juan in the Village by JANE DELYNN

Our Lady of the Flowers by JEAN GENET

The Well of Loneliness by RADCLYFFE HALL

The Line of Beauty by ALAN HOLLINGHURST

Tales of the City by ARMISTEAD MAUPIN

'Brokeback Mountain',
Close Range: Wyoming Stories by ANNIE PROULX

The Story of the Night by COLM TÓIBÍN

A Boy's Own Story by EDMUND WHITE

Oranges Are Not the Only Fruit
by JEANETTE WINTERSON

Top Ten Cult Classics

Whether exploring controversial subject matters such as drug abuse and the breakdown of society, or experimenting with unusual and sometimes challenging writing styles, all the books listed below dispense with conventionality and, as a result, have earned themselves a strong cult following. Release the rebel in you and read on . . .

The New York Trilogy by PAUL AUSTER

Cocaine Nights by J. G. BALLARD

Naked Lunch by WILLIAM BURROUGHS

Generation X by DOUGLAS COUPLAND

A Million Little Pieces by JAMES FREY
(originally published as non-fiction; the author
was later revealed to have fabricated chunks of the text)

On the Road by JACK KEROUAC

Bright Lights, Big City by JAY MCINERNEY

The Dice Man by LUKE RHINEHART

Valley of the Dolls by JACQUELINE SUSANN

Fear and Loathing in Las Vegas
by HUNTER S. THOMPSON

Midnight's Children

Salman Rushdie

Published 1981 / Length 463 pages

'To understand just one life, you have to swallow the world.'

Born at the very instant when India achieves its independence from British colonial rule, Saleem Sinai is a cipher for a country, a 'mirror-of-the-nation'. This central metaphor permeates Rushdie's magic-realist tour de force. Sinai's family, too, is an extension of his nation; both are bound together into 'imagined communities' by shared memories. Making masterful leaps through time and space, the novel is dizzying in scope. Rushdie splits narratives into fragments and forces them to fuse again in endlessly surprising ways. Pace is not necessarily his strong point, but the tension is sustained throughout with the device of count-downs to momentous events. The luxuriant exuberance and lusty ambition of Rushdie's unashamed love affair with words also keeps you hooked. He is fearless about diversions, parentheses, and what look at first like irrelevances. A refreshing concession to the reader's sense of exhaustion as we plough through this imposingly dense doorstopper comes in the shape of Padma, an impatient listener constantly demanding clarification and driving the narrative along with her 'what-happened-nextism'.

Reader's opinion

'*The Tin Drum*, *100 Years of Solitude* and *1,001 Nights* all rolled together, this allegorical, encyclopaedic journey of a book left me wondering if I was reading a story of personal events and private beliefs or the public history of post-colonial India.' – SYLVIA, 57

Discussion points

● The narrator talks the reader through the writing process as if we are by his side. What do we gain from being party to his reflections on what he is writing?

- Do you think Rushdie believes we should try to 'think our way out of our past'? How do the characters cope with the past's presence in every corner of their lives?

- What might Rushdie be trying to tell us by underlining the physical limitations of Saleem's body? And why the recurring metaphor of physical fragmentation?

BACKGROUND INFORMATION

- The formal partition of India occurred on 15 August 1947. Hundreds of thousands of people died as massive population exchanges took place across the new border between Hindu-majority India and Muslim-majority Pakistan.

- In 1989, Rushdie was forced to go into hiding when he was made the subject of a fatwa, exhorting his killing for blasphemy, by Iran's Ayatollah Khomeini, in response to Rushdie's depiction of the Prophet Muhammad in *The Satanic Verses*. The fatwa controversy was renewed in June 2007 when Rushdie was knighted.

- *Midnight's Children* won the 1981 Booker Prize, and went on to be named the 'Booker of Bookers', the best book to have won the prize in its twenty-five-year history, in 1993.

SUGGESTED COMPANION BOOKS

- *Heart of Darkness* by JOSEPH CONRAD (see page 52) – a classic study of the way colonial rule corrupted both colonizer and colonized.

- *The Inheritance of Loss* by KIRAN DESAI (see page 56) – when Desai won the Booker for this 2006 novel, the judges noted Rushdie's influence. How does Desai's perspective on the colonial legacy compare to Rushdie's?

The Catcher in the Rye

J. D. SALINGER

Published 1951 / Length 192 pages

The Catcher in the Rye is narrated by Holden Caulfield, an American teenager who is recovering from a nervous breakdown. Caulfield relates a series of events that occurred a few months earlier, following his expulsion from prep school. They include awkward encounters with an ex-girlfriend, a prostitute, a couple of taxi drivers and a former teacher. Holden seeks human contact, but he feels alienated by the hypocrisy and 'phoniness' of the adult world. It's only through regressing to childhood, as represented by his younger sister Phoebe, that Holden finds solace. The colloquial first-person voice of *The Catcher in the Rye* is brilliantly realized and utterly convincing. As Salinger sustains the monologue, he vividly evokes the confusion of becoming an adult in a world of uncertain values. Published in the early fifties, the novel was as important as rock-and-roll music and the films of James Dean in developing the modern notion of the teenager.

READER'S OPINION

'Salinger captures the cynical teen very well. I knew that this was supposed to be a "modern classic", but what surprised me when I read it was how funny it was. Although there wasn't much of a plot, I got hooked and finished the book quite quickly.' – STEVE, 24

DISCUSSION POINTS

- Is Holden ever guilty of 'phoniness' himself?
- How do Holden's attitudes to the adults and children in the novel differ? What does this say about his opinion of adulthood and childhood?

- The narration takes place a few months after the events described. How does this affect Holden's account of them?
- What is Holden's attitude to sex?
- Do you think Holden has made a full recovery from his breakdown? What kind of an adult do you think he'll become?

BACKGROUND INFORMATION

- *The Catcher in the Rye* has sold over 60 million copies to date and remains Salinger's only full-length novel. Following its success, Salinger retired and lived as a recluse.
- Mark Chapman was found to be carrying a copy of the book when he was arrested for murdering John Lennon.
- The novel has been banned by many US libraries and schools on the grounds that it contains swearing and sexual subject matter.
- Despite many offers from Hollywood, Salinger has always refused to sell the film rights to the novel.
- The novel's title comes from Holden's misquotation of the Robert Burns poem 'Coming Through the Rye', and is an allusion to baseball.

SUGGESTED COMPANION BOOKS

- *The Adventures of Huckleberry Finn* by MARK TWAIN (see page 208) – an earlier American coming-of-age classic.
- *The Great Gatsby* by F. SCOTT FITZGERALD (see page 72) – a major influence on Salinger.
- *The Bell Jar* by SYLVIA PLATH (see page 168) – a semi-autobiographical novel that also gives a troubled teenager's account of the fifties, set partly in New York.
- *The Curious Incident of the Dog in the Night-Time* by MARK HADDON – a first-person account of a teenager with Asperger's syndrome trying to make sense of the adult world.

Drowning Ruth

CHRISTINA SCHWARZ

Published 2000 / Length 276 pages

A tense, mysterious novel filled with secrets, *Drowning Ruth* is the tale of spinster Amanda Starkey and her family, set just after the First World War in rural, often bleak Wisconsin. Amanda's sister Mattie is dead – Mattie's only daughter Ruth left motherless – but no one is clear what happened the terrible night she died, or who is to blame. No one, that is, except Amanda. As Ruth grows up under the intense and watchful eye of her steadfast aunt, their sheltered lives eventually intertwine with characters who were best avoided, bringing about an inevitable and irrevocable climax. In haunting, neat prose, the novel explores the familial ties that bind (and sometimes choke); the art of manipulation; sibling rivalries and jealousies; and the dangers of obsessive love. Intermittently told from the perspectives of Amanda and Ruth, the story unwinds against the backdrop of Nagawaukee Lake, a landscape so atmospherically conjured that it seems almost like a character itself. The book is populated with unsympathetic yet charismatic people, as Schwarz masterfully reveals lies and misguided loyalties with expertly judged pace.

WHAT THE CRITICS SAID

'A sense of doom ahead grips the reader from the first page of this assured and dense debut. The repressed emotions and small-town society morals are a winning formula, but Schwarz's real achievement is in matching the complexities of her plot with vivid characters.' – *The Scotsman*

DISCUSSION POINTS

● Cowardice is a theme in the book. Who do you think is the bravest character?

- Schwarz presents two generations of three friends. What are the similarities and differences between these trios? Does history repeat itself?
- Do any of the characters deserve their fate?
- What was the effect of switching the narrative viewpoint? Did it mean the story was more reliably told?
- Is Amanda a murderess?

BACKGROUND INFORMATION

- The book was selected for Oprah's Book Club in 2000.
- Schwarz said she was originally inspired to write the book from her memories of a reclusive neighbour – 'I romanticized the tragic life that had made her want to shut herself away' – though the story then took on a life of its own.
- The film rights have been optioned by *Nightmare on Elm Street* director Wes Craven.

SUGGESTED COMPANION BOOKS

- *Sins of the Fathers* by Susan Howatch – another book that plays around with the narrative perspective.
- *The Pilot's Wife* by Anita Shreve – a modern-day story concerned with family secrets and living a life in ignorance of the truth. Shreve publicly supported *Drowning Ruth*, describing it as 'mesmerizing'.
- *Liars and Saints* by Maile Meloy (see page 138) – a book that perhaps explores what might have happened if Mattie's plan had worked.
- *Notes on a Scandal* by Zoë Heller (see page 104) – the all-powerful effect of a manipulative central character.

The Lovely Bones

ALICE SEBOLD

Published 2002 / Length 328 pages

On 6 December 1973, fourteen-year-old Susie Salmon is raped
and murdered by a man from her neighbourhood. This, and the
devastating impact these brutal events have on those who loved
her, form the narrative of *The Lovely Bones*. Susie herself is our
guide, telling her story from heaven, as she looks down on the
people she has been forced to leave behind, closely following
their lives over several years as they respond to her ever-present
absence. The book draws on many genres: part thriller, as we
wait to see if her killer will be caught; part supernatural mystery;
part coming-of-age story; and part redemptive novel. Exploring
myriad themes including loss of innocence, the collective conscience of community and the intricacies of family dynamics, it
is a sparsely written yet powerful story – marrying murder with a
strange hopefulness and peace, giving a controversial vision of
heaven, and providing one of the most memorable opening
chapters in recent literary history.

READER'S OPINION

'Written from the unique viewpoint of a murdered teenager,
The Lovely Bones is one of the most moving and compelling
books I have ever read. Marred only by an overtly sentimental
ending, this book is both riveting and thought-provoking.
Highly recommended.' – HELEN, 32

DISCUSSION POINTS

- The book is suffused with imagery of articles encased in glass
  jars – the penguin in the snow globe, the ships in bottles. Of
  whom or what are these images symbolic?
- Why do you think Sebold created the character of Lindsey?

- Many (British) critics have accused the book of being saccharine and overly sentimental. Do you agree with them? Would the book have been as commercially successful if it described a different afterlife?
- Is Mr Harvey evil to the core? Does Sebold present him as possessing human fallibility, or is he just a monster?
- Think about the incident towards the end of the novel, when Sebold breaks her own rules about heaven. Do you think this plot development was successful? Was it dramatically necessary?

BACKGROUND INFORMATION

- The book is the most successful US debut since *Gone with the Wind*. Many attribute its triumph to a post-9/11 America, where the idea that the dead don't leave us was balm to the national grief.
- Sebold began *The Lovely Bones* in 1996, but then put it on hold while she wrote *Lucky*, a memoir about her own rape at eighteen, as she didn't want to contaminate Susie's story with polemic.
- The book won the inaugural *Richard & Judy* Best Read Award at the British Book Awards in 2004.

SUGGESTED COMPANION BOOKS

- *Lucky* by ALICE SEBOLD – compare the author's fictional and autobiographical treatment of violent crime.
- *The Bell Jar* by SYLVIA PLATH (see page 168) – exploring the feelings and imagery of alienation; paralleling characters' stories.
- *To Kill a Mockingbird* by HARPER LEE (see page 130) – examining crime and the community.
- *Lolita* by VLADIMIR NABOKOV (see page 152) – getting inside the mind of a paedophile.

The Bookseller of Kabul

ASNE SEIERSTAD

Published 2003 / Length 276 pages

This fictionalized account of Norwegian journalist Asne Seierstad's four-month stay with a Kabul family in spring 2002, just months after the start of NATO's war in Afghanistan, is an engrossing read. The author insists that the family of our aptly named protagonist, Sultan, is not 'typical'; she resists giving Western readers a template for 'understanding' a country that appeared on the radar of most only after the US-led invasion. The label of 'fiction' slips somewhat, though, when Seierstad inserts, through the voice of one unforgettable character, the full text of a Taliban radio broadcast banning music, dancing, the education of women and (bizarrely) pigeon-rearing. Meanwhile, her anger at the subjugation of women in Afghan society comes through loud and clear. She is adamant that the Taliban are not responsible for this remorseless, everyday oppression. Women suffocate in domestic spaces, she argues, because of Afghan tradition: the combination of commercial necessity and ingrained structures of familial obligation make marriages into 'business deals' in which women are bartered for. Her reflections on the roots of female victimization are deeply serious, but the book remains insightful, simple and often humorous.

READER'S OPINION

'The power and transparency of the reportage made me feel as if I, rather than Asne Seierstad, had just spent four months in Kabul with the Khan family. I was gripped by the immediacy of her experiences.' – CAROLE, 59

DISCUSSION POINTS

● To what extent does Seierstad preserve her journalistic objectivity? How even-handed is her treatment of men and women?

- Why do you think the author uses dust as a central image of women's oppression?
- Is Seierstad too much of an outsider to examine Afghan culture as anything other than a voyeur? Or does she provide a bridge to an unfamiliar culture?
- Did you spy any hope for change in the book?
- Sultan insists that he wants to preserve Afghan culture and heritage. Given some of the more problematic sides to that culture that we see in the book, do you agree that preserving tradition for its own sake is a good thing?

Background information

- The real-life bookseller, Shah Mohammed Rais, has threatened to write his own account of events, telling the world's press that Seierstad's depiction of Afghanistan was 'false and salacious'.
- A war journalist by training, Seierstad has also written *With Their Backs to the World* (2000) about Serbia, and *A Hundred and One Days: A Baghdad Journal* (2005) about life in Iraq immediately before, during and after the US-led invasion in 2003.
- The book was selected for the 2004 *Richard & Judy* Book Club.

Suggested companion books

- *Fahrenheit 451* by RAY BRADBURY – describes a regime that burns books, and its contempt for learning and imagination.
- *Nineteen Eighty-Four* by GEORGE ORWELL (see page 158) – depicts a controlled society where covert love affairs are conducted through notes and barely perceptible signs. The Ministry of Love echoes the surreal Ministry of Morality.
- *The Handmaid's Tale* by MARGARET ATWOOD (see page 20) – set in a dystopia where gender is used as a basis for social control.

Fortune's Rocks

ANITA SHREVE

Published 2000 / Length 453 pages

In this rite-of-passage story, which begins on the cusp of a new century in 1899, Olympia Biddeford is fifteen years old and being educated at home in New England by her publisher father. One of his author friends, John Haskell, a forty-year-old married man with four children of his own, visits them one summer and – unexpectedly and shockingly – embarks on a brief but passionate affair with Olympia. From this point on, Olympia's life is changed for ever. Shreve's nineteenth-century-style prose is eloquent and believable, beautifully evoking the time, place and attitudes, and the detail is meticulous. Though the pace occasionally slows a little, this does not detract from the overall experience of reading what is a polished, moving and assured novel.

WHAT THE CRITICS SAID

'*Fortune's Rocks* boasts distinguished literary ancestors, Nathaniel Hawthorne's *The Scarlet Letter* for one, and Edith Wharton's *Summer* for another . . . these novels conjure up the stiflingly unrealistic morality of America's highly puritanical New England . . . [and] focus on the irrevocable effects that a few moments of sexual passion can set in motion, not just in one couple but in their entire surrounding community.' – *The Washington Post*

DISCUSSION POINTS

● Do you think there's a feminist message in this book? If so, is that message compromised by the knowledge that Olympia relies on her family's wealth and station in her attempts to overcome her situation?

- Is the novel enhanced or spoiled by the type of ending it has?
- The novel has been likened to *Wuthering Heights*, with Olympia and John replacing Catherine and Heathcliff. How well does this comparison stand up?
- Does Shreve succeed in creating a believable chemistry between the two lovers?
- Do you think the writing style that Shreve intentionally adopts is successful? How would the story differ if told in a more modern literary style?

Background information

- As well as writing fiction, Shreve is a well-known writer on women's studies and psychology. *Fortune's Rocks* is her seventh novel and the first, chronologically, in what is described as 'an informal trilogy' with *The Pilot's Wife* (1998) and *Sea Glass* (2002).
- Shreve says she loves writing in nineteenth-century prose, having first done so for *The Weight of Water* (1997), which was shortlisted for the 1998 Orange Prize for Fiction.

Suggested companion books

- *After You'd Gone* by MAGGIE O'FARRELL – describes a psychological journey through one woman's past following a traffic accident.
- *Wuthering Heights* by EMILY BRONTË – depicts two lovers tied to each other through adversity; and disparate reactions to, and the long-term impact of, grief.
- *Sea Glass* by ANITA SHREVE – the setting is 1920s New Hampshire; a couple's attempt to maintain their marriage against a backdrop of labour conflict.
- *The Pilot's Wife* by ANITA SHREVE – a woman's struggle with private grief in the glare of public interest in modern-day New England.

We Need to Talk About Kevin

LIONEL SHRIVER

Published 2003 / Length 400 pages

We Need to Talk About Kevin has become a classic choice for book clubs worldwide: controversial, shocking and psychologically intense, this is a novel that polarizes opinions and is guaranteed to spark a lively debate amongst its readers. The bare plot bones alone reveal that this is not a comfortable read. In a series of letters to her absent husband, Eva Khatchadourian tells the story of their teenage son, Kevin, who one fatal Thursday murders seven of his fellow students and two high-school workers in a cold-blooded massacre. The novel follows Kevin's life story from his birth to the present day, where he resides in prison, tracing Eva's increasing alienation from her son as the events build up to their terrible (and unexpected) climax. At its heart, the book poses a number of disturbing questions about the nature of evil, the alienation of modern American society, and the nature-versus-nurture debate. Above all, it explores the last great taboo of motherhood: the bonds and limitations of 'unconditional' parental love.

WHAT THE CRITICS SAID

'Is the author suggesting that human evil is the product of imperfect mothering? Far from being a free and frank investigation into the truth about motherhood, is this, in fact, a Republican morality tale proffering dark warnings about the price of women's liberation?' – *The Guardian*

DISCUSSION POINTS

- Who do you think was ultimately to 'blame' for Kevin's actions? Could the final outcome have been prevented?
- How reliable did you find Eva as a narrator? Did you always

believe her version of events and did you find her
sympathetic?

- The epigraph to the book is a quote by Erma Bombeck: 'A
child needs your love when he deserves it least.' Do you think
the events of the novel bear this out?

- Lionel Shriver herself does not have children. Do you think
this is relevant in her depiction of motherhood?

BACKGROUND INFORMATION

- *We Need to Talk About Kevin* won the 2005 Orange Prize for
Fiction.

- Lionel Shriver was born in the US and has lived in Israel,
Nairobi, Bangkok, Vietnam and Belfast, now dividing her
time between London and New York. *We Need to Talk About
Kevin* is her seventh book.

- In summer 2003, *The New York Observer* reported that *Kevin*
had gained a word-of-mouth feminist following. The novelist
Pearson Marx stated: 'This book has given women permission
to feel things that they weren't allowed to feel.'

SUGGESTED COMPANION BOOKS

- *Vernon God Little* by D. B. C. PIERRE (see page 166) –
another recent novel exploring the American high-school-
killings phenomenon, though from a very different
perspective.

- *Madame Bovary* by GUSTAVE FLAUBERT – the archetypal
ambivalent mother.

- *Unless* by CAROL SHIELDS – a middle-class American
mother struggles to cope with her daughter's withdrawal from
society.

- *Nineteen Minutes* by JODI PICOULT – examines the impact
on personal lives and the wider community when a high-
school massacre occurs.

On Beauty

Zadie Smith

Published 2005 / Length 445 pages

Smith's celebrated ability to capture the zeitgeist makes *On Beauty*, a double-headed saga about the families of two rival academics, an absolute must-read. It is a chattery book whose high-achieving characters draw you into their social world, where they spar and jostle for position as intellectual and sensual beings. The family scenes are deftly portrayed: Smith's sketches of spats and reconciliations in these close-knit collectives of independently minded individuals are lively and acutely observed. But the book is also interested in love and desire, exploring men's need to be admired and women's need to dedicate their lives to someone else. As it tracks the collision of these male and female desires in the neurosis-fuelled hothouse of Wellington College, New England, *On Beauty* becomes, at times, sad and even squalid reading. Still, Smith is unquenchably witty, sprinkling the text with irreverent observations and deadpan asides, and ventriloquizing young and old with a well-tuned ear for idiom that allows her to migrate effortlessly across registers. *On Beauty* may teeter on the brink of being mercilessly cool, but it definitely has a heart.

WHAT THE CRITICS SAID

'[T]he kind of book that reminds you of why you read novels to begin with . . . a catalogue of human [follies], but none are depicted without compassion and a certain measure of delight in their vibrant particularity and underlying universality.' – *Salon*

DISCUSSION POINTS

- Is Smith more comfortable with some of her characters' 'voices' than others? How can you tell?

- Is Howard's behaviour both 'boring' and 'obvious', as his daughter Zora tells him? What makes him do what he does?
- Do Clare Malcolm and Victoria (Vee) Kipps have any redeeming features?
- Why do the Belsey women dedicate their lives to men? In the light of these characters, how do you react to Smith's decision to dedicate the book and 'my life' to her husband in the acknowledgements?

BACKGROUND INFORMATION

- *On Beauty* is, roughly, a modern reworking of E. M. Forster's 1910 novel *Howards End*.
- It won the 2006 Orange Prize for Fiction.
- The choice of title links the book to an influential work of philosophy, *On Beauty and Being Just*, by Elaine Scarry.

SUGGESTED COMPANION BOOKS

- *The Secret History* by DONNA TARTT (see page 198) – perhaps the archetypal campus novel, with larger-than-life characters made self-conscious by their youth and inexperience, as much in love with learning as with themselves and with each other.
- *Small World* by DAVID LODGE – another widely admired example of the 'campus literature' genre, which satirically portrays the petty self-absorption of academics competing for recognition.

Sophie's Choice

William Styron

Published 1979 / Length 632 pages

Stingo – the name an obvious near-match for 'Styron' – is a fledgling novelist in search of a story. Living in cheap rented lodgings in New York in 1947, he finds one unexpectedly in the dark history of post-war émigré Sophie Zawistowska, who inhabits the room above. Playing third wheel in her frenetically intense love affair with American-Jewish Nathan Landau, Stingo becomes a willing confidant to this vivacious, voracious and gorgeous Pole, who is weighed down by the secrets of her unmasterable past.

Styron balances the story of Sophie's guilt with the sexual awakening of his alter ego, handling these unsettlingly juxtaposed genres with remarkable tact. *Sophie's Choice* is in some ways simply a coming-of-age novel whose events play out over one long, hot Brooklyn summer. But it is in its extraordinarily fresh look at the aftermath of suffering for Holocaust survivors that *Sophie's Choice* excels. Tackling a subject most modern novelists would steer well clear of, Styron exposes the facile knowingness with which Americans used the 'catchwords' of the genocide – Auschwitz, Dachau, Buchenwald – without comprehending them. He forces us to look hard at a tragedy that seems absolute and listen to a story about events that appear to demand silence.

What the critics said

'A harrowing meditation on the destruction of innocence.' – *The New York Times*

Discussion points

- Does Stingo's early search for a narrative worth writing make his decision to tell Sophie's story seem exploitative?
- How successfully does Styron weave chunks of history and

theory into his tale? Is he concerned with creating compelling fiction or educating his reader?

- Do you think Styron is right to insist on penetrating the 'impenetrable evil' of Auschwitz? Is speaking, or silence, the proper response to tragedy of such vast dimensions?

BACKGROUND INFORMATION

- *Sophie's Choice* was adapted for the big screen in 1982. The film version starred Meryl Streep and Kevin Kline; although Styron reportedly insisted he had had Bond girl Ursula Andress in mind as he wrote. Nevertheless, Streep won an Oscar for her performance.

SUGGESTED COMPANION BOOKS

- *The Shawl* by CYNTHIA OZICK – this very short and very stark tale deals with one Holocaust survivor's memory of a horrific instance of 'man's inhumanity to man'.
- *If This Is a Man* by PRIMO LEVI – a Holocaust memoir unmatched in its detail, humanity and unerring moral sense.
- *The Drowned and the Saved* by PRIMO LEVI – reflects on the survivors' legacy of guilt, exploring complicity and collaboration in the 'grey zone' and mounting a powerful appeal for the Holocaust to be remembered in a truthful, accurate way.

Perfume

Patrick Süskind

Published 1985 / Length 272 pages

Perfume tells the extraordinary tale of Jean-Baptiste Grenouille, who is born on a heap of fish guts at a fish stall in the sweltering heat and stinking squalor of eighteenth-century Paris. Abandoned by his mother, and later orphaned, the young Grenouille is notable for two strange characteristics: from birth, the boy is completely odourless, but conversely he has a heightened sense of smell. An odd character whose weird demeanour makes him a social outcast, his life is dominated by sampling the many smells of Paris, which he catalogues in his own internal library. After finding work with a second-rate perfumier, he transforms the business thanks to his natural olfactory creativity. However, Grenouille's fascination with the aromas of the city takes a more sinister turn when he embarks on a murderous pursuit to source the most perfect human scent, which he intends to recreate and use for himself to compensate for his own lack of odour. Disturbing, but vivid, *Perfume* is a horrifying, fantastical work of historical fiction, utterly unique in its subject matter, which makes for a compelling read.

READER'S OPINION

'I was blown away by this book. Not only was the sheer originality of the story amazing, but the descriptions used to convey Grenouille's incredible sense of smell and the filth of eighteenth-century Paris were enthralling. A bizarre but intriguing tale.' – MARK, 32

DISCUSSION POINTS

● Does Grenouille inspire pity or hatred in you? Is he a protagonist for whom it is possible to have sympathy?

- Is Süskind successful in conveying to the reader the many different smells that bombard Grenouille's every waking moment? What sort of imagery does the author use?

- In addition to Grenouille's lack of smell, what other human characteristics does he appear to be missing?

- How much is his mother's early rejection of him to blame for Grenouille's apparent detachment from society? Or is this a result of society's negative response to the odourless young man?

- Is Grenouille the victim of circumstance, or is he simply an evil, inhuman individual?

BACKGROUND INFORMATION

- *Perfume* is Patrick Süskind's debut novel and was originally published in German as *Das Parfüm* before becoming an international bestseller.

- It was awarded the prize for Best First Novel by the *Frankfurter Allgemeine Zeitung*, but the author turned it down because he did not wish to accept awards for his writing.

- His next work of fiction, a novella entitled *The Pigeon*, was similarly unusual: a man's sanity is threatened by the presence of a pigeon roosting outside his front door.

SUGGESTED COMPANION BOOKS

- *The Invisible Man* by H. G. WELLS – a brilliant young scientist makes himself invisible, but things don't work out quite how he intended.

- *The Strange Case of Dr Jekyll and Mr Hyde* by ROBERT LOUIS STEVENSON – explores the mysteries of creating a potion to separate good from evil in humans.

- *Frankenstein* by MARY SHELLEY – another tale of a scientific experiment gone wrong.

The Secret History

DONNA TARTT

Published 1992 / Length 640 pages

The Secret History is a psychological suspense thriller concerning the lives of a group of Classics students who are insular and glamorous, but ultimately murderous. The novel's narrator, Richard Papen, spends an unremarkable working-class childhood in Plano, California, before being transported to the elite Hampden College in Vermont. Here he becomes obsessed with a group of eccentric students and their professor, Julian Morrow. Eventually managing to gain access to the coterie, Papen finds that darker forces than he could ever have imagined govern this new circle of friends – sweet-natured twins Charles and Camilla Macauley, effete Francis Abernathy, scholarly Henry Winter and jovial Bunny Corcoran. Perceiving the modern world through the literature and philosophy of ancient Greece, the classmates embark upon a path that sees them abandon social strictures for Bacchanalian freedom – and the results are macabre. Through the first-person narrative of Papen, Tartt draws on Greek tragedy and crime fiction to create a fast-paced, absorbing, modern cult classic.

READER'S OPINION

'This book was a great read. I was instantly gripped by the plot and by Tartt's dense descriptive style, which was promisingly dark, brooding and full of mystery. The narrator's engaging voice and Tartt's characterization of the central figures cemented my enjoyment – believable as individuals and fascinating as a group, I wanted to be in their gang.' – KIERAN, 23

DISCUSSION POINTS

- Critic A. E. Scott deemed *The Secret History* a 'murder mystery in reverse' due to its use of the prologue, which reveals the murder, victim, location and perpetrators. What do you think is the purpose and effect of such a device?

- The characters of Henry, Francis, Charles, Camilla and Bunny were ill-received by some critics, who regarded them as flat stereotypes. Do you think this is a fair assessment?
- What, in your opinion, is the role of fate in the novel?

BACKGROUND INFORMATION

- Tartt began writing *The Secret History* while she was an undergraduate at Bennington College, Vermont, and the novel took eight years to complete.
- *The Secret History* is dedicated to Bret Easton Ellis, a close friend of Tartt's, and one of the first people to whom she showed the manuscript. It was through Ellis that Tartt was introduced to literary agent Amanda Urban, who accepted her as a client.
- The novel's first print run on its publication in the US was a massive 75,000 copies, compared with the usual 10,000. Even so, demand for the book was so great that additional printings had to be ordered.

SUGGESTED COMPANION BOOKS

- *The Little Friend* by DONNA TARTT – a twelve-year-old girl sets out to solve the murder of her brother ten years previously.
- *The Rules of Attraction* by BRET EASTON ELLIS – life on campus is saturated with drugs, sex and debauchery at a liberal arts college in New Hampshire.

The Colour

Rose Tremain

Published 2003 / Length 368 pages

The Colour is an utterly compelling story of a quest for fulfilment, absolution and gold. Joseph Blackstone, his new wife
Harriet, and his widowed mother Lilian have come to mid-
nineteenth-century New Zealand to start over. Once the flimsy
civilization of Christchurch has been left behind, however, they
find themselves with a fight on their hands – both to wrest control of this new land they have come to, and to prevent the past
from breaking down their fragile relationships with each other.
While Harriet embraces and indeed begins in small ways to tame
the wild environment, Joseph and Lilian soon lose faith in their
endeavours to build a home, and former shames continue to dis-
able them. Then Joseph sees 'a flicker of colour in the grey mud'
of the creek and takes on a new hope and a new secret. For that
colour is gold. By the time Joseph leaves to join the gold rush that
is gathering momentum on the other side of the Southern Alps,
Harriet has begun to look to her own needs – until events force
her, too, to undertake the arduous journey to the goldfields.

WHAT THE CRITICS SAID

'Tremain's novel is about the power of transformation. Do we
choose a quiet life over a daring and difficult one? What does it
feel like to be unlovable? Do we understand our darker sexual
selves? [. . . A]n acute study of ambition, guilt and repressed
desire.' – *The Observer*

DISCUSSION POINTS

- In the book, man and nature are frequently at war with one
  another. What do you make of Dorothy's belief that
  'inevitably we make a small world in the midst of a big one.
  For a small world is all that we know how to make'?

- When Joseph begins his search for gold, he literally succumbs to a debilitating fever. Discuss the changes that the gold rush has effected in the town of Christchurch and how this affects Lilian.

- Consider the story of Edwin and his Maori nurse Pare. What does this add to the book?

- Discuss the character, relationships and fate of Joseph Blackstone.

- What do we think of Harriet? Is her relationship with Pao Yi convincing?

BACKGROUND INFORMATION

- *The Colour* was shortlisted for the 2004 Orange Prize for Fiction.

- Tremain was moved to write about the mid-nineteenth-century gold rush in New Zealand when she saw the flimsiness of the prospectors' tools in a museum there.

SUGGESTED COMPANION BOOKS

- *The Virgin Blue* by TRACEY CHEVALIER – a haunting tale in which a woman's disturbing nightmares are suffused by the colour blue, leading her to trace the fate of her French Huguenot ancestors.

- *Villette* by CHARLOTTE BRONTË – another young woman flees from an unhappy past to make her way in the world; the book similarly examines the lot of middle-class women in the Victorian period, and questions whether marriage is a better option than working as a governess.

- *The Mosquito Coast* by PAUL THEROUX – seeking to escape the evils of modern living, inventor Allie Fox turns his back on civilization and attempts to build a new life for his family in the Honduran rainforest.

The Story of Lucy Gault

WILLIAM TREVOR

Published 2002 / Length 240 pages

The story begins in 1921, in a remote rural location in Ireland during the Troubles. A Protestant family finds itself increasingly under threat from arson attacks amidst the general civil unrest sweeping across the country, which has forced innocent people to abandon their properties and flee to safety. Eight-year-old Lucy Gault lives with her Anglo-Irish soldier father and English mother, and is desperate not to leave the family home. But when her father accidentally shoots a young troublemaker trespassing on his land, her parents decide that it is impossible for the family to remain in their house, for fear of reprisals. Uncomprehending of the seriousness of her parents' situation, Lucy decides to take matters into her own hands, and as a result of a single childish act, tragedy ensues and changes the dynamic of the Gault family for ever. Contemplating themes of guilt, forgiveness, loss, suffering, human fragility and the consequences of fate, the agonizing heartbreak underpinning *The Story of Lucy Gault* will prove impossible to forget.

READER'S OPINION

'A compelling and poignant tale about the ramifications of our actions. Trevor weaves together so many human emotions in a wholly empathetic and subtle way that our sympathies for the main characters are instantly aroused and we ourselves start to mourn for the damaged lives of Lucy and her parents.' – SARAH, 28

DISCUSSION POINTS

● If Lucy's parents had been less inclined to believe the worst and had avoided jumping to the wrong conclusion before every avenue had been explored, do you think the central tragedy of the story could have been averted?

- Whose guilt was the greater: Lucy's, or that of her parents? Who do you think was most responsible for the events that developed?
- How much of a role did the historical context of the book (particularly the Troubles) play in the situation that unfolded?
- In the aftermath of the tragedy, do you think that Lucy's parents dealt with their grief as individuals, rather than confronting it in unity?
- Why did Lucy treat Ralph in the way she did? Was it perhaps as a penance for her earlier sins?

BACKGROUND INFORMATION

- *The Story of Lucy Gault* was shortlisted for both the Booker Prize and the Whitbread Prize for Best Novel in 2002.
- William Trevor is the author of numerous prize-winning novels, including *Fools of Fortune* and *Felicia's Journey*, and is also a prolific writer of short stories.
- A native of Ireland, where many of his works are set, Trevor was granted an honorary knighthood in 2002 for his inestimable services to literature.

SUGGESTED COMPANION BOOKS

- *Mourning Ruby* by HELEN DUNMORE – explores the twin subjects of guilt and grief associated with family tragedy.
- *Atonement* by IAN MCEWAN (see page 134) – a tale of how a single action can produce life-changing consequences.
- *Crime and Punishment* by FYODOR DOSTOEVSKY – examines the action of attaining salvation through suffering.

Top Ten Sci-Fi Books

Science fiction is perhaps the most imaginative genre of all literature, and for that reason alone it's worth sampling the crème de la crème of this category. The fantastic worlds created in such books are not only remarkable for their inventive detail, however – they also have much to convey about human nature.

The Boat of a Million Years by POUL ANDERSON

Darwin's Radio by GREG BEAR

The Martian Chronicles by RAY BRADBURY

Do Androids Dream of Electric Sheep?
by PHILIP K. DICK

Solaris by STANISLAW LEM

The *Canopus in Argos* series by DORIS LESSING

20,000 Leagues Under the Sea by JULES VERNE

The War of the Worlds by H. G. WELLS

The Humanoids by JACK WILLIAMSON

The Day of the Triffids by JOHN WYNDHAM

Top Ten Chilling Reads

If you and your book club have the courage, why not scare yourselves witless with these ten chilling reads? 'Horror' is a literary
genre with ancient roots: from folklore to *Frankenstein*, ghost
stories to Stephen King, unsettling narratives are enduringly
popular and all too memorable. Terrify yourselves with these top
tales – if you dare . . .

The Exorcist by WILLIAM PETER BLATTY

Red Dragon by THOMAS HARRIS

Ghost Stories of an Antiquary by M. R. JAMES
(a collection of short stories)

Host by PETER JAMES

The Stand by STEPHEN KING

Tales of Mystery & Imagination by EDGAR ALLAN POE
(a collection of short stories)

Frankenstein by MARY SHELLEY

The Strange Case of Dr Jekyll and Mr Hyde
by ROBERT LOUIS STEVENSON

Dracula by BRAM STOKER

Ring by KOJI SUZUKI

Marrying the Mistress

JOANNA TROLLOPE

Published 2000 / Length 336 pages

Breaking up is never easy, especially in the case of sixty-two-year-old Guy Stockdale, who leaves his wife of forty years, Laura, for a newer, younger model three decades his junior, with whom he's been having a secret affair for the past seven years. Matters are further complicated by the impact his decision has on his two grown-up sons, Simon and Alan – especially when Laura puts increasing pressure on the family to take sides. In the meantime, Merrion, Guy's mistress, has to face the problems of coming to terms with the Stockdales, with the growing realization that she can't just have Guy without his family. *Marrying the Mistress* examines the fallout from Guy's decision, the complexities of family relationships, and how misunderstandings and lack of communication can be passed on through the generations. It looks at what is expected of families in a crisis . . . although what is expected is not necessarily what happens.

WHAT THE CRITICS SAID

'For a woman with two marriages behind her, Joanna Trollope is unexpectedly indulgent to men. Indeed, the main unreality of this novel is her attribution of complicated emotions to her male characters. Men who take off with girls half their age could quite often give you a robustly simple explanation of their actions – one that never features here.' – *Sunday Herald*

DISCUSSION POINTS

- Lack of communication and misconceptions play a large part in this book. How do they affect each of the main characters and their relationships with each other?
- What impact do those outside the Stockdale family have on

what happens? Consider Mrs Palmer, Wendy and Colin in particular.

- The three mothers all have very different relationships with their children. How do you think these steer the events in the book?
- Do your sympathies change during the course of the novel? If so, why?

BACKGROUND INFORMATION

- Trollope's books have been dubbed 'Aga sagas'. Her response to this has been: 'The name itself indicates a provincial cosiness, and is patronizing of the readers. A lot of what I write into the books is bleak and challenging, but I will be the Queen of the Aga saga to my dying day. It's jolly annoying, but it is better than being the Queen of Hearts.' (*The Guardian*, 2003)
- Trollope has been married twice, and has two daughters, two stepsons, and grandchildren. She now lives on her own in London.
- The Victorian novelist, Anthony Trollope, is a distant ancestor.
- Trollope also writes historical novels under the pseudonym Caroline Harvey, which is a combination of her grandparents' first names.

SUGGESTED COMPANION BOOKS

- *Howards End* by E. M. FORSTER – examines how an unexpected marriage affects a family.
- *On Beauty* by ZADIE SMITH (see page 192) – a modern-day reworking of *Howards End*, exploring similar relationships in a contemporary setting.
- *The Pursuit of Love* by NANCY MITFORD – describes the complexities of family dynamics.

The Adventures of Huckleberry Finn

MARK TWAIN

Published 1884 / Length 369 pages

Often thought of as the quintessential American novel, *The Adventures of Huckleberry Finn* is the tale of a thirteen-year-old boy named Huckleberry Finn and his escapades on the Mississippi River. The story is told through Huck's eyes, and words in the text are often spelt as Huck would spell them, lending this adventure story a lighthearted tone. However, beneath this carefree veneer are deeper themes, including racism. When Jim, Widow Douglas's slave, finds out that he is going to be sold and separated from his family, he runs away to try to find a way to the Free States. He and Huck team up on a raft and Huck vows to help Jim escape. Along the way, the pair encounter con men, thieves and feuding aristocrats, who all try to unbalance the equal terms by which Huck and Jim live peacefully on the raft. Ultimately, Huck's journey downriver is symbolic of his personal development, as he realizes that society's way is not necessarily the only way; and this is Twain's message to America.

READER'S OPINION

'It's the kind of book you can enjoy on whatever level you feel like. It deals with heavy themes, but they never become overpowering, so you can just enjoy the adventure.' – MARK, 23

DISCUSSION POINTS

- The Notice at the beginning of the book pokes fun at those who will try to find a moral – but by including this, does Twain insist that the book is more than just an adventure?

- Is the book racist or anti-racist? Are Huck's comments and actions knowingly prejudiced, behaving as society expects in order to trick it, or does he really believe these things?

- The contrast between Huck and Jim's small society on the raft and that on the banks of the Mississippi is striking. What is Twain trying to say about Southern values?
- Does the ending of the novel undermine any moral messages?

BACKGROUND INFORMATION

- The novel was banned for being subversive when first published; it was thought to present ideological perspectives that would go against traditional Southern values.
- The American Civil War was fought between 1861 and 1865. One of the aims of the Northern States was the emancipation of slaves in the South. *Huckleberry Finn* was published in 1884, two decades after the war had been won by the North and the Reconstruction – the integration of freed slaves back into society – had begun. Though the book is set before the Civil War, it is often thought to be a comment on conditions for blacks even after the abolition of slavery.
- Twain was once a riverboat pilot on the Mississippi. His real name was Samuel Langhorne Clemens; Mark Twain was a pseudonym. The name comes from the cry of the leadsman measuring depth from the bows of a riverboat: 'By the mark, twain!'

SUGGESTED COMPANION BOOKS

- *The Adventures of Tom Sawyer* by MARK TWAIN – the companion book that precedes *Huckleberry Finn*.
- *Swallows and Amazons* by ARTHUR RANSOME – similar themes of children's adventures from an English perspective.
- *A Portrait of the Artist as a Young Man* by JAMES JOYCE – focuses on similar issues of growing up through shirking the traditions and conventions of society.

Rabbit, Run

John Updike

Published 1960 / Length 320 pages

Harry 'Rabbit' Angstrom is a former college basketball hero with a pregnant wife and a three-year-old child. The setting is 1950s small-town America and the young marriage is not a success. Rabbit has a dead-end job and his wife spends her afternoons watching television and drinking whisky. Rabbit is restless.

The couple argue over a trivial matter and, on a whim, Rabbit walks out on his family with a romantic notion of waking up by the Gulf of Mexico. The reality is more prosaic, as he moves in with a part-time prostitute. The novel looks at how close family and the supposed pillars of the local community react to Rabbit's absence and infidelity, and also at how Rabbit himself justifies his actions. Both the book's subject matter and language were considered shocking upon publication. Over the years, that power to shock has faded, but there remain some graphic and loveless descriptions of lust, and a tragic conclusion. As a result, *Rabbit, Run* is a bitter, compelling and claustrophobic book.

What the critics said

'*Rabbit, Run* is a tender and discerning study of the desperate and the hungering in our midst. Updike has a knack of tilting his observations just a little, so that even a commonplace phrase catches the light.' – *The New York Times*

Discussion points

- How effective is the minister, Jack Eccles, at convincing Rabbit to return to his wife? What do you think Jack's motives are?
- How much blame do you attribute to Janice for Rabbit walking out on his family?

- What is Rabbit looking for?
- Does the book still retain some power to shock?
- The text is written in the present tense. What impact does this have on the storytelling?

BACKGROUND INFORMATION

- Updike wanted to create a counterpoint novel to Kerouac's *On the Road*, saying in a feature article for Penguin Modern Classics: 'What happens when a young American family man goes on the road – the people left behind get hurt.' His book examines those repercussions.
- Several of the more sexually explicit passages were cut from the original text, but restored in subsequent editions.
- *Rabbit, Run* is followed by three more 'Rabbit' novels, all published at the start of subsequent decades.

SUGGESTED COMPANION BOOKS

- *Rabbit Redux* (1971), *Rabbit is Rich* (1981) and *Rabbit at Rest* (1990) by JOHN UPDIKE – the three 'Rabbit' sequels.
- *Something Happened* by JOSEPH HELLER – a dark study of the American dream and a failing marriage.
- *The Catcher in the Rye* by J. D. SALINGER (see page 180) – also deals with the alienating effect of modern life.
- *On the Road* by JACK KEROUAC – the flip side of *Rabbit, Run*.

The Color Purple

ALICE WALKER

Published 1982 / Length 244 pages

'I'm poor, I'm black, I may be ugly . . . but I'm here.'

The Color Purple follows the life of Celie, a young African-American woman living in Georgia in the 1900s, and her battle to endure and ultimately prevail against three oppressive forces: racism, sexism and poverty. The novel opens by launching the reader into an onslaught of traumatic and violent events that see a weak and submissive Celie marrying the abusive widower Mr —, or Albert. Celie's emotional, sexual and spiritual development is nurtured by the large community of women which clusters around her – including her husband's mistress, Shug Avery, a free-spirited blues singer – until Celie has grown into a strong, independent woman. The novel's language and content is unflinching as it deals with incest, rape and exploitation. Yet Walker is concerned to balance her narrative with a message about the redemptive power of love that enables both abused and abuser to break out of their destructive cycle. She also communicates an essential need for dignity and inner strength – required in order that the characters may change and grow.

READER'S OPINION

'Some people say they find the book depressing, but I disagree. Celie's quest to find love, creativity and spiritual peace is uplifting and universal. The violence is still shocking and upsetting, but I think the book has some humour, too.' – BELLA, 28

DISCUSSION POINTS

- Walker says that for her, the book 'remains a theological work examining the journey from the religious back to the spiritual'. What evidence can you find to support this? What does the colour purple symbolize?

- *The Color Purple* is an epistolary novel: the story is told through letters and diary entries. Why do you think Walker used this structure? What are its advantages and disadvantages?

- What do you think Walker is saying about identity? Consider the representation of colonial Africa and think also about the significance of names in the novel.

- Many readers are disturbed by Walker's portrayal of black men. Would you agree that the black male characters are depicted as one-dimensional abusers? If so, why?

BACKGROUND INFORMATION

- *The Color Purple* won the 1983 Pulitzer Prize and is among the top-five reread books in America.

- Steven Spielberg directed a film adaptation of the novel in 1985; it starred Whoopi Goldberg as Celie.

- Walker lived in Mississippi during the civil-rights movement's most active phase, and was a leading campaigner for black women's rights. She is permanently blind in one eye, as is the character of Sofia.

SUGGESTED COMPANION BOOKS

- *I Know Why the Caged Bird Sings* by MAYA ANGELOU (see page 16) – corresponding themes of racism, violence and sexuality. How are Marguerite's struggles similar or different to Celie's?

- *Beloved* by TONI MORRISON (see page 142) – another novel exploring the harrowing life of an African-American woman.

- *Narrative of the Life of Frederick Douglass, an American Slave* by FREDERICK DOUGLASS – a classic work in the slave narrative tradition. Consider whether oppression and emancipation mean the same thing for Frederick and Celie.

The Night Watch

SARAH WATERS

Published 2006 / Length 474 pages

A fast-paced yet tender story of people coping with present troubles and the demons of their past, *The Night Watch* follows the fortunes of three women and one man in 1940s London: Kay, a tomboy and former ambulance driver who now seems lost in Civvy Street; troubled Helen, whose insecurities drive her to desperation and jealousy; Viv, stuck with a soldier in a relationship that's run its course; and young Duncan, who cannot leave the mistakes of his past behind.

The narrative starts in 1947, a few years after the end of the Second World War, and moves back in time to conclude with its beginning in 1941, tracing the origins of the characters' grief, personalities and stories. Their paths intersect in a vividly evoked war-ravaged London, full of ever-changing bombed streetscapes, personal struggles and choices made under oppressive circumstances. Gripping and emotionally resonant, *The Night Watch* explores the uneasy transition to peace that follows wartime.

READER'S OPINION

'I enjoyed the story and felt Waters created the atmosphere of the period very well; the protagonists didn't seem like twenty-first-century characters transplanted back in time like they often do. Telling the story "backwards" was an interesting idea and created a different type of tension – instead of wondering what was going to happen or if so-and-so would survive, you concentrated on how they got there and what had brought them there.'
– ANNE, 56

DISCUSSION POINTS

● Why do you think the author chose a reverse chronological

structure to tell the story? What is the effect on character development, the reader's reaction to events, and the ending?

- What opportunities and challenges does the setting provide for the characters and the plot?

- Duncan describes Kay as looking like 'one of those women . . . who'd charged about so happily during the war, and then got left over'. How accurate a description do you think this is? What are the differences between female and male experiences of war in the novel?

- The story follows three women and one man. What is Duncan's role in the book? Why is he included?

BACKGROUND INFORMATION

- This is Sarah Waters's fourth novel. *The Night Watch* marked a departure from her usual setting of Victorian England and was also her first novel to be written in the third person.

- The novel was shortlisted for both the Booker Prize and the Orange Prize for Fiction in 2006. It won the Lambda Literary Award 2007.

SUGGESTED COMPANION BOOKS

- *Night Shall Overtake Us* by KATE SAUNDERS – four female friends live through the First World War; loss and fragile relationships during wartime.

- *The End of the Affair* by GRAHAM GREENE (see page 88) – set in the same bleak post-war years, but written by an author who lived through the time, this was one of the novels that Waters said provided inspiration for *The Night Watch*.

- *Small Island* by ANDREA LEVY (see page 132) – post-war London's transition to peace seen from the perspective of Caribbean immigrants and their neighbours.

Brideshead Revisited

Evelyn Waugh

Published 1945 / Length 331 pages

During the Second World War, Charles Ryder, an army officer, is billeted at Brideshead Castle – but it is not his first visit to the stately home of Lord Marchmain (whose family name is Flyte). Through Ryder's first-person narrative, Waugh transports his reader to Oxford University twenty years previously, where Charles is befriended by the eccentric but glamorous Lord Sebastian Flyte, the wayward youngest son of the aristocratic family. Always accompanied by his teddy bear, Aloysius, and with an exclusive group of friends, Lord Sebastian cuts a dazzling figure around Oxford. Charles is taken to the family's seat at Brideshead Castle where, despite Sebastian's protestations, he begins to forge life-changing relationships with the Flytes. The family are Roman Catholic, and their faith informs every aspect of their lives. Charles is destined to re-encounter the Flytes over the years in a series of formative events that give shape to his social and religious conscience. Waugh himself summed up *Brideshead Revisited* most succinctly when he wrote that the novel is concerned with the 'operation of divine grace on a group of diverse but closely connected characters'.

What the critics said

'First and last an enchanting story, *Brideshead Revisited* has a magic that is rare in current literature. It is a world in itself, and the reader lives in it, and is loath to leave it when the last page is turned.' – *Saturday Review*

Discussion points

● The first part of the novel is titled '*Et In Arcadia Ego*', a Latin phrase that can be translated as 'I [Death] am even in

Arcadia [paradise]'. In what ways do you think Waugh makes his reader aware of decay and mortality in the early stages of the novel?

- The exact nature of Charles and Sebastian's relationship has been the subject of much critical scrutiny. Are they simply platonic friends, or does Waugh imply a physical relationship between them? In what ways does Charles's relationship with Julia mimic and/or diverge from this?

- What do you think of Waugh's treatment of Roman Catholicism and divine grace, particularly in the novel's final chapter and its study of Lord Marchmain?

BACKGROUND INFORMATION

- *Brideshead Revisited* is a *roman-à-clef*: many of the characters are identifiably based on Waugh's real-life acquaintances.

- *Time* magazine included *Brideshead Revisited* on its list of 'All-Time 100 Novels'. Waugh himself referred to the work on several occasions as his 'magnum opus'.

- Waugh's knowledge of Oxford University stemmed from his own experience there as an undergraduate at Hertford College, where he graduated with a third-class degree in Modern History. When asked if he had competed in any sport for his college, he famously replied, 'I drank for Hertford.'

SUGGESTED COMPANION BOOKS

- *A Handful of Dust* by EVELYN WAUGH – a satire chronicling the breakdown of a marriage.

- *The Beautiful and Damned* by F. SCOTT FITZGERALD – a glamorous couple of the jazz age hit hard times and face harsh realities.

- *Love in a Cold Climate* by NANCY MITFORD – follows the loves and losses of its upper-class heroines in pre-war Paris and London.

Mrs Dalloway

Virginia Woolf

Published 1925 / Length 213 pages

Mrs Dalloway is an important example of experimental modernist literature. Eschewing the conventions of the novel and using a stream-of-consciousness narrative, Woolf attempts to describe the workings of the human mind by illustrating all the thoughts of her characters. The book centres on Clarissa Dalloway, a politician's wife, a mother and a wealthy member of post-war London society, for a single day in June 1923 as she prepares to host a party. As the plot develops, Clarissa's unhappiness becomes clear, as she contemplates the past and the future as represented by her various guests. Septimus Warren Smith, a former soldier suffering from shell shock, highlights the social legacy of the First World War; his narration also offers an insight into mental illness. Septimus and the other characters' thoughts converge to form a holistic view of Clarissa as the book builds to its climax. Though *Mrs Dalloway*'s form and style are challenging, the sheer breadth of Woolf's themes and the dexterity with which she renders human emotion make for a thoroughly rewarding read.

READER'S OPINION

'This novel incorporates such a diversity of characters that there's never a dull moment. The possible autobiographical implications in the character of Septimus make for a genuine insight into the mind of the author.' – SHERRI, 22

DISCUSSION POINTS

- Woolf's use of the stream-of-consciousness technique raises the question of whether a book can realistically describe human thought. Which features of Woolf's writing aim for realism?

- How does Woolf's passion for metropolis come across in her descriptions of London? How do her feelings about post-war society present themselves?
- What do you make of the parallels between Septimus and Clarissa, and the ways in which they relate to Woolf herself? (See BACKGROUND INFORMATION.) Is Woolf trying to suggest anything about the treatment of mental illness?
- Do you think the female characters in the book – especially Sally Seton, Elizabeth Dalloway and Clarissa herself – are a comment on feminism? If so, in what way(s)?

BACKGROUND INFORMATION

- Published in 1925, *Mrs Dalloway* depicts London after the First World War, as women strove for fairer treatment and a more influential place in society.
- The novel started life as two short stories. Despite being an experiment in narrative and style, it was one of Woolf's biggest commercial successes.
- Woolf struggled with mental illness throughout her life. The parts of the novel concerning Septimus were based on her own experiences; she saw them as an exorcism of her demons.

SUGGESTED COMPANION BOOKS

- *The Hours* by MICHAEL CUNNINGHAM – tells the story of three women influenced by *Mrs Dalloway*.
- *Ulysses* by JAMES JOYCE and *Saturday* by IAN MCEWAN – both employ stream-of-consciousness narratives and the events described take place over the course of a single day.
- *The Bell Jar* by SYLVIA PLATH (see page 168) – deals with similar issues of mental breakdown and the pressures of womanhood.
- *A Room of One's Own* by VIRGINIA WOOLF – an essay about the constraints on women in post-First World War society.

The Shadow of the Wind

Carlos Ruiz Zafón

Published 2004 / Length 504 pages

A self-consciously literary thriller, translated from the original Spanish, *The Shadow of the Wind* paints a convincing picture of Barcelona during Franco's rule, riddled with paranoia and suspicion. It tells the story of Daniel Sempere, a young man who finds a copy of *The Shadow of the Wind* by Julián Carax while exploring a mysterious library at the heart of the city. Daniel spends the following years trying to track down the enigmatic Carax and uncover the truth behind his disappearance, while his own love life gradually begins to mirror Carax's doomed romance. An aggressive member of Franco's secret police and an inscrutable stranger in a black leather mask also take an interest in Carax's story, and before Daniel knows it he becomes involved in political intrigue as he draws closer to the truth. Flashbacks slowly illuminate the tragic history behind the author of *The Shadow of the Wind*, before both the reader and Daniel Sempere are propelled towards the thrilling climax, and some surprising revelations.

READER'S OPINION

'A charming love story, but with an original element – I couldn't help being pulled into the characters' world of intrigue and tragedy in post-Civil War Barcelona. I was even inspired to go to some of the sites from the book on a visit to the city, just to prolong the memories. Well worth a read.' – HANNAH, 32

DISCUSSION POINTS

● There are many parallels between the lives of Daniel Sempere and Julián Carax scattered throughout the book. What effect do these have? At what point do their lives diverge, and how is this divergence achieved?

- *The Shadow of the Wind* is both the title of this novel, and the title of the novel within it. What is 'the shadow of the wind'?
- There are various portrayals of evil in the book, some absolute, some dependent on circumstance. What do you think Zafón is trying to say about the nature of evil?

BACKGROUND INFORMATION

- *The Shadow of the Wind* is the first in a series of four novels that Zafón has planned, all set in Barcelona.
- After Miguel de Cervantes's *Don Quixote*, *The Shadow of the Wind* is the most popular Spanish novel ever. To date, it has sold over 7 million copies worldwide.
- The book was selected for the *Richard & Judy* Book Club in 2005.

SUGGESTED COMPANION BOOKS

- *The Name of the Rose* by UMBERTO ECO – another literary thriller based around a fictional book.
- *Winter in Madrid* by C. J. SANSOM – a different perspective on the Spanish Civil War.
- *The Count of Monte Cristo* by ALEXANDRE DUMAS – features political prisoners, vengeance and hidden identities.
- *Oracle Night* by PAUL AUSTER – books within books; fiction engaging with reality.

The Book Thief

MARKUS ZUSAK

Published 2005 / Length 584 pages

Set in Nazi Germany during the Second World War, and narrated by the Grim Reaper himself, *The Book Thief* tells the story of Liesel Meminger, and through her explores the misery and the legacy of the Holocaust. Within the first few pages, Liesel witnesses the death of her brother and is sent to stay with a foster family, her own parents having been removed to a concentration camp for harbouring communist tendencies. Her foster parents are Hans and Rosa Hubermann, whom Liesel gradually begins to love and respect as she uncovers their many hidden qualities. Living with the Hubermanns in Himmel Street, on the outskirts of Munich, she comes to know many of the local characters, some of whom will change her life for ever. She forms a strong friendship with Rudy Steiner, a local boy who is obsessed with American athlete Jesse Owens, but an even stronger relationship gradually develops with Max Vandenburg, a Jewish runaway who spends the daytime hiding in the Hubermanns' basement. As Liesel grows up, the war begins to affect every aspect of her life, until finally tragedy finds its way to Himmel Street.

WHAT THE CRITICS SAID

'Zusak's Death is a cumbersome trope; he doesn't solve the narrative problem so much as betray the author's failure to recognize its nature. He is verbose and vapid, sentimental and simplistic, pleased with his own facile ironies, constantly inviting the reader's connivance in tediously familiar postmodern games.' – *The Sunday Times*

DISCUSSION POINTS

● Why do you think Zusak chose Death as the narrator for this story? What effect does his omniscient viewpoint have on the telling of it?

- The narrator describes Liesel as 'one of those perpetual survivors – an expert at being left behind'. Is this an adequate description of her?

- What is the meaning of Max Vandenburg's *The Word Shaker*? Is it fair to say that it's the most significant of Liesel's books?

- Given that we hardly see Liesel's original family within the confines of the novel, why do you think Zusak made her a foster child?

BACKGROUND INFORMATION

- Markus Zusak is half Austrian and half German, although he was born and raised in Sydney, Australia.

- *The Book Thief* was inspired by the wartime tales Zusak's mother told him, including the story of a child giving bread to Jewish prisoners that appears in the novel.

- The novel won the Teen Book Award 2007 from the Association of Jewish Libraries, and also triumphed in the Young Adult/Children's category of the 2006 National Jewish Book Awards.

SUGGESTED COMPANION BOOKS

- *The Diary of a Young Girl* by ANNE FRANK – a Jewish girl's real-life diary, written during the Nazi occupation of Holland.

- *Reaper Man* by TERRY PRATCHETT – a different fictional representation of Death.

- *Everything Is Illuminated* by JONATHAN SAFRAN FOER – tackling the Holocaust from an unusual perspective.

Acknowledgements

Grateful thanks to Lionel Shriver for providing the elegant Foreword; and to book club member Ana Sampson for the Introduction, and the initial idea for the book. Thanks are also due to the entire team at Michael O'Mara Books, who assisted with the list of books included and many other elements of this title.

In addition, gratitude is due to the following contributors, who supplied the detailed entries on the 100 recommended titles. In alphabetical order:

Stephen Blake, Tim Collins, Dan Coxon, Helen Cumberbatch, Ben Davies, Lindsay Davies, Sarah Drinkwater, Juliana Foster, Eilidh Franses, Mike Gregory, Kate Gribble, Cathryn Harker, Maureen Harker, Andrew John, Paul Julien, Shelley Klein, Nicky Lander, Anna Marx, Chris Maynard, Sophie Middlemiss, Ben Olins, Kate Parker, Andy Pickford, Tess Read, Victoria Reed, Ana Sampson, Liz Scoggins, Anita Sethi, Rochelle Sibley, Eve Tindale, George Ttoouli, Helen Weaver, Sally Wilks, J. A. Wines, Steven Wines, and Jenny Wood.

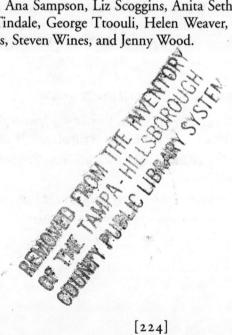